THE LORDS OF
SEPTEMBER
J. Charles Egan

Fulton Books, Inc.
New York, NY

First originally published by Fulton Books 2015

ISBN 978-1-63338-027-1 (paperback)
ISBN 978-1-63338-028-8 (digital)

Printed in the United States of America

Take the journey with me from a kid in a small farming community in the Midwest to the jungles of Southeast Asia, where I am proud to say I served with the U.S. Army Special Forces. Follow me as I share some of my own personal experiences during the war in Vietnam—some funny—others not so.

I was educated in Catholic school and I must give the nuns credit for saving my life. After all, dodging the yardstick was not much different than dodging bullets. When the war ended, I moved to Nevada where I attended the university. I am married and now living in Florida with my wife and three small dogs. I am proud of the young men and women of today who have put their lives on hold for this great country of ours. Many have returned, others were not so fortunate.

If you find yourself on any of these pages, know that all of us have experienced the same things: the fear of not coming home alive, fighting for survival and watching as our friends fell around us. Hold no animosities, they will destroy you. Keep your emotions in check and never the forget the sacrifice.

THE LORDS OF SEPTEMBER

Midnight in the Garden

I remember the plane landing. It was my first trip to Vietnam. The roar of the engines as the pilot, on a scheduled run did his best to clear air space and get the ship on the ground before we began to take fire…it was a war zone. He and his crew were bringing in a load of replacement personnel and the crew knew from experience not everyone on board would make it back. They were congenial, and personally I do not think they were given enough credit for their efforts. Some, like myself, it was their first time country as well. Only difference was I didn't much give a shit, others, just kids for the most part were obviously shaken by the fact it was all real now—no more bullshit. Once the plane stopped and the doors opened all hell broke loose. If they were trying to hit the plane or just scare the hell out of everyone It was working. I thought to myself I had not been there long enough to piss anyone off. Just imagine what it's going to be like six months from now. It won't be safe within fifty miles of me unless you have a death wish.

Not one soul on that plane was ready for what was to come. There were mixed emotions when the plane departed Seattle/Tacoma (SEATAC) airport—not anymore!

As kids from small towns and farms we led sheltered lives and trauma was missing a dance on Saturday night. Maybe losing a girl-friend, but no one was ready for this. No one ever is.

Over the many years time has allowed us to share, some would become restless souls, being careful never to stay in one place to long.... searching, confused, running, what? We now find ourselves in a "war zone"! The past is never far behind, the end is where all things someday meet. It is the bridge in the middle that leads to September.

Do we ever come to terms with life?....No. We must go on how-ever. We must survive. We do what we feel is right. That's nature. It makes little difference in the waning years of our lives. Our battle is now with September. You cannot go back, that was yesterday, today takes that away, there is only tomorrow, and if we are fortunate there will another day and the process will begin anew. You can not change the past. Live with what there is, love what you have and cherish the one person who has always been there. Never compare one thing with another, only let certain things serve as a gentle reminder of other days. Speak of the past if you must with reverence and hold only yourself in awe. The road of life is a beautiful journey and at times harrowing. It is a road we must all take to the bridge we all must one day cross.

Follow along as we break the code in this fact based fictionalized account of one mans journey thru his life.

Do not leave quietly nor in despair, and gently, ever so gently, ride the soft warm winds of time into the light....to that house in September, not made with hands.

DEDICATED TO MY FATHER

Sleep well September Soldier
Look down from the pillow of the clouds only to smile. Know
that you have done well. Dwell if you Must, only on the things
in life that made you smile. Let no one tear this under.
Do not weep when September comes.
It comes for everyone. The crystal bridge awaits.

PROLOGUE

As kids we wonder what it would be like to be in the shoes of our father...our hero, the one who always had a story to tell of something, things in his life that on occasion seemed disturbing, especially of his war experience that he described ever so vividly, on more that one occasion. Sometimes just to his friends, then to our mother or other close loved ones who would listen and seemingly were brought to tears by the tales that were related...as we all listened. He was seeking solace. It was his way of reaching out for understanding. He had his family and that is all that mattered to him. What was this war he spoke of?

We would place ourselves in our hero's shoes and say quietly that someday we would do the same thing, never realizing the horrors that would accompany us on that journey...to the real battlefield. We never lose sight of the dream of one day becoming that soldier, quietly hoping that it will not be over before we get there.

We were children then, some barely old enough to attend school. Others in second or third grade. They seemed like our leaders as we played out the same scenes that our fathers had spoken of...only theirs was for real, ours was on the playground at school or in the park on weekends. Oh, so long ago.

One thing is certain, we can never go back. There is only today and always remember, tomorrow will take that away. We will all say that none of our sons or daughters will go thru what we did…in some cases that may come true, but is that what we really want? We must let them make the little mistakes we did growing up it is part of life. We will help them to avoid the major pitfalls and pick them up, again and again. In some cases it will be with a soft caress and some kind words, others not so gentle, but try we must. The road is long and arduous, fraught with danger. There will be some among us that will not make it. There is no explanation no matter how hard we try, it simply happens. Go to the wall for them if you must, as many times as necessary, then back away or it will destroy not only ourselves but others around us.

It was difficult growing up in our house. The war (WWII) for my father had not been over that long and he was still living with his ghosts. When Korea came along he was drafted back into the service. Nothing he could do…he tried. There were four of us kids when that happened.

I remember the day he left, Mom was doing what she always did… keeping her mouth shut, and just standing with a blank look on her face, that look of fear, her kids alongside and a tear in her eye knowing in her heart that things were only going to get worse. No food, no money and no support from her family, either morally or financially—after all she gave birth to me. At the time I was considered a "bastard". My plane landed about three months early and back in the day that was a BIG no no! I was the embarrassment of everyone in the small minded family of good little Catholics we lived in at the time. Human Erectus Mortal Sin!! The apple and the snake fable!

I never did understand why as a kid, I was the object of such ridicule and scorn. Why should I? I was a kid. It took a few more years to figure out what a religious bigot was!

My Grandmother was a religious bigot, a real horses ass and she took it out on my mother, her own daughter every chance she got and never missed taking a shot at me when no one was around. The exception however was my grandfather. He tended to me when no one was around and if anyone said anything he simply said…"Shut Up"! "Mind your own damn business"! That statement would put fear in all around at the time. He was big Irishman with a heart of gold and a temper like a rattlesnake. He tried to keep peace in the family but he could only take so much. My grandmother was afraid of him…and rightfully so, she never stopped nagging. She would always push him right to the edge and then back off about the time he was getting ready to launch her ass across the room. There were times when I wished he had. I never trusted her. She was devious. A religious zealot! She had a sister who was worse than she was. People were afraid to be in the same room when that old bat came around. She always had a fist full of prayer beads that she passed out and expected everyone to fall on their knees kiss her ass and pray for the little orphans in South America and ALWAYS found it necessary to remind us that she just sent money to them, while her own people (us) sat living in abject poverty—she simply did not care! Then she would leave, but always reminded us that we would get our reward in heaven. I had no idea what that meant but we were hungry now! Maybe she thought we would eat the damn prayer beads. All this however was punishment for my mother…and of course me…the one who left the launching pad three months early! I was an object—not a kid, an object! I was always referred to as him, you or he!

The problem in that era was, if a girl got that way, they were on their way to hell. There were exceptions however. Later on in years some priests were running off with one of the Nuns, and this was common place. It was a sin to even mouth any of the other things that may have taken place. God knows where I would have ended up had I mentioned hearing of the shenanigans…just remain silent!! Now brother, that's politics, and I've heard it called a lot of things, but politics!!? Nothing was ever said about my weird ass uncle who lived at home all his life—he had been tossed out of the service and dear old Grammie thought that was a secret. Everyone in town knew it. He was way to loose in the loafers for them army boys. Nothing was ever said about that. One pit-fall in dear ole Grammies life is all the old bat could handle. She didn't want anyone to know about uncle pixie.

I guess being a bastard wasn't that bad after all!!

Nothing was ever going to change that however, and my mother would pay dearly for what was perceived to be the great sin back in the day. All thanks to the moral high ground, and pay she did—till the day of her death at the age of thirty eight having child number eleven. The little baby (later named Jeff) died with her. I can only imagine that had he lived there would have been another Joel in the family—a soft hearted, intelligent clown!

11

Someone once said, there is no tragedy in life like that of losing a child—things never got back to the way they were for our Dad. One can only imagine losing both a child and a spouse on the same day and it would not be long before another would follow.

CHAPTER ONE

(The Odyssey Begins)

Our mother managed to eke out a survival system for us while Dad was in Korea…She begged!

No help from the church and especially from any of the congregants, who were probably afraid if they were to assist us in any way or they would go straight to hell.

One pissin little town full of over zealous Christians, drunks and draft dodgers! The ones who did not fit in any category were so damn dumb the military begged them to stay home. Friday and Saturday nights were always big nights for the Catholics, etal. There was standing room only in the bars. When the bars closed, half of them would end up in the wrong beds, in the wrong houses! Maybe they were not so dumb after all! Saturday was to sober up, hopefully by noon, work a little and head for the bars again. When they closed it was the same as the Friday night ritual. The Catholics were great ritualists. I know. I used to be an altar boy—imagine that!! It didn't last long after I found out where the Priest hid the altar wine. You only get caught once sucking on that jug and it's strike three!

Ah yes, now I know why God invented Sunday. It's a day of rest!?

I don't recall that Dad wrote home while he was away—I'm sure he probably did…our mother just never said anything. Who would listen. When Dad finally came home from Korea he had changed. Even our mother was afraid of him.

As kids we never understood why, without reason, he would fly into a rage striking out for no apparent reason. I don't think he did either. On reflection I feel he was absolutely as mad as anyone could be regarding the absence of any type of assistance from our Mother's family while he was gone. No need to look to Dads family—all he had was his mother and she was a drunk. God bless her, she never pretended to be anything else. She lived about seven or eight miles from us and on occasion when I was a kid I got a chance to visit her. It was fun…they lived in an old house with a big attic full of junk she collected over the years and would always let me rummage thru it. I would always get a big stinking wet whiskey smelling hug and kiss when I arrived and the same when I left, except she would always give me some kind of shriveled up apple to take along. She really meant well. Never asked me how I got there and never asked How I was going to get home, just said goodbye and shut the door. Maybe she thought I lived across the street. By the time I left she was ready for a nip or two. I'm not sure when she died, but years later she fell out of her chair and they buried her. The only other relative was Dad's step father. A really great guy. Grandpa Wes (Holmes). He was a big Irish Cop in the local village. Carried a small gun and a blackjack. He kept order…his way. I was a lucky Irish kid—I had two fantastic (Irish) grandfathers!

There were ten kids in our family before it was all over and each of us had our own very distinct personalities, especially my brother Joel. He was a nut! Which by the time I left home was driving our Dad insane. Joel and his buddy Jim—the two of them were like the lone ranger and Tonto. The two of them had a way of keeping Dads nerves very keen!

Our Mother was a very humble person. She never had anything she could call her own and never placed herself above the needs of her kids.

Dad was the worker and at that time it was how things were. The man worked and the Wife stayed home…it was another time. It seems hard to believe that things could ever have been that simple. We grow up oh-so-fast.

I remember one thing my mother told me, " never grow old before your time"! That little phrase stuck with me for the rest of my life.

A year later she was dead. Dead at the age of thirty eight having sibling number eleven. Just what we needed!

I was seventeen at the time and had been in the military for three months already. I enlisted the day I graduated from high school.

The first time I recall her saying that little phrase was when I was being shot at in Vietnam. We were in a bad situation and I just knew it would be my last night on earth. I just did not want to die so far from home. So what the hell was I doing there? It is what I had always dreamed of when I was a kid—being a soldier and being in a war just like my Dad. I only wish he had explained that I might die face down in some mud hole, ten thousand miles from home with a bullet in my head. He always encouraged that I should join the military. It seemed more like an obligation to him rather than a choice for me—and of course make him proud, hopefully. I just wanted to get out of the damn town I was raised in. I was beginning to feel trapped and yet I knew there was something else outside the hills of my little village. Actually, I feared living there—it was conform, ask no questions, go to church, get a job on some farm and just fade into natures painting.

Dad really wanted me to be a priest…you know, just like all good catholic families do when they have a spare son. Sacrifice him on the altar of yore and look good in the beady little eyes of the community Gods!

"Take him he's yours"! Kind of like the sacrifice of old when they would put the first born on some rock and….well you get the idea. And all this just for sucking on the church wine when I was an altar boy. Not for me! I'll do penance another way! I just didn't think giving up my life and especially girls was an appropriate punishment for the crime. I'll take my chances in the Military. What he didn't know was that if he had not signed for me to go into the service (I was only seventeen), I probably would have left and joined the foreign legion. He might have gone with me!

My Dad always wanted me to be in the service, just not the army like he was. He almost insisted that I join the Navy after I told him the Priesthood was out, and he picked himself up off the floor—Which I did!

I did not know what to expect in the Navy but I did learn that it consisted of a bunch of Gray boats that bobbed around on this great expanse of water known as the ocean and on occasion we would pull into some foreign port, drink our brains out, get (our) pipes cleaned in some whore house and six months later we were sitting in some dry-dock in the states again, living like hobo's and it would be six months of dust, dirt, rust and paint, then back out to sea again!

Not for me!

When I got out of the Navy, I joined the Army. Once again my Dad nearly passed out when I showed up at home in an Army uniform! He always accused me of being a little different but this was more than he could take! Apparently he was unaware you could do that (join another branch of service) and asked me what the hell I thought I was doing? After a brief explanation he (said) he understood—at least I think he did. He still seemed apprehensive about the whole thing. I know he checked it out after I left town to see if this was acceptable! I guess I was the only one who had ever done this—at least to his knowledge.

All of my brothers and sisters were still at home. Dad had arranged for someone to come in while he was working and assist with the care of the little ones and do some of the cooking…when he got home she would leave.

This went on for a number of years and as time went by another of the kids would leave home.

Dad pretended not to notice that the family was shrinking and the little house we were raised in was getting larger. I'm sure he shed more than a tear or two each time but he never allowed his feelings to be shown overtly. I think Dad feared that someday after we were all gone he would then be left by himself. The one thing he feared. He never remarried. There were several ladies in his life. They all made the same mistake—they would try and get too close to the kids and when this happened they were down the road. Joel would recognize immediately when some floozy was trying her best for an easier life at the expense of the kids. None of them were ever to succeed in that venture. All of them had bad drinking and smoking habits. Dad was no saint, but he was not about to tolerate some lush around his family and with Joel's help—he succeeded.

There were turbulent times and strife over the years but he would deal with each situation as it came along. One of the things that effected him most as years went on was in November of 1967 when one of our sisters (Jeri) was killed in an automobile accident (barely sixteen). This also had an extremely traumatic effect on our Sister (Jennifer). The two of them were inseparable and to this day she still shows the signs of her loss in little ways. We were all effected by the loss of our sister, but it was different with Jennifer—they were more like twins.

Seemed like Dad was just beginning to get over the loss of our mother when this occurred. I never realized it at the time, but the man was a rock—he always knew what he had to do next and he did it. He was an extremely intelligent man and because of it was somewhat feared, and hated by his own peer group. He would not be told what or how to do things. There was always some half wit willing to give advice.

He was deeply traumatized by this event in his life but he tried never to show his emotions around anyone. Dad drank more than usual after this but he never let it effect his performance at work. Sure, people would talk…but that's just what small minded people do and they exist in every town in this country—large and small. The individuals who had the most influence on Dad were his two best friends—to the day of his death. Doc and Pinky. They know who they are. We should all be so lucky to have someone like these two as true friends. The three of them were practically inseparable. My brother Joel referred to them as the "Three Kings"!

Joel is my personal hero. Absolutely one of the most intelligent people I have ever known.

He's the type of person that everyone would like to have as a friend, but never cross him and never say anything adverse about his family. That's hallowed ground.

I remember one time in Vietnam when we were taking pretty heavy fire in a patrol situation—hit and run mostly but it was uphill and I just knew I had finally stepped in more shit than I could shovel.

I began thinking about my Brother Joel.

He could always make you laugh no matter the situation.

I remembered him telling me about how he ended up in the Seminary. Joel and his best friend (for life) Jim. After about two years of not being priestly material and relegated to mowing ten acres of lawn more times that the local landscaping service, they decided one day to make their way home. Fire up the mowers, make one pass around the building, recon the area and cut a straight path to freedom. Park the mowers in the weeds and hitch a ride home. Four hundred miles. When they arrived, there was the not so welcome party waiting. After the inquisition Joel decided he would venture into the Military—where it was safe. Jim stayed home and went to work in his Dad's grocery store (it didn't last long) but it was the beginning of a new start for the both of them. Funny just what goes thru a persons mind when they are under stress and the dying part seems imminent.

Son-of-a-bitch we were starting to take fire from above our location—we were in deep poop and I knew it. I left half of my people to ambush the patrol chasing us from below and decided to go head long into the fire from above. Luck was on our side, we had not lost one man to this point and I was going to make damn sure it stayed that way. Now I was pissed. Call for air support and let them take the top of the hill apart. Bad idea. It was daylight and my team was dressed just like the V.C., (an operational thing) You can bet I would have lost every man and probably got myself shot for the trouble—fuck it! Work this one out. Then I get the word from my interpreter that the team below finished up. They killed six. That's the extent of what was chasing us. Now I was really pissed. When we finally regrouped, instead of going straight up or backing down we made an end run around them. Went about one hundred yards to the east, then proceeded to go back up the side of that damn mountain. When the firing stopped I guess they thought that we were all dead and made the mistake of coming down to look. In the process we had mounted the top and made a straight run at the bastards—we managed to kill what was left of their element. Four more. Don't think about it just radio in our situation and call for an extraction....only make damn sure the choppers know who we are and how we were dressed. The damn door gunners on the gun ships would shoot at anything. Everything in that area was free game for the choppers. Bunkhouse this is eight seven. Advise when you have communication with the choppers and get the frequency they want us on. Bunkhouse eight seven this is your friendly extraction service. You got any wounded? No. Go ahead, over. Understand you are on a hill side...can you make it to anyplace a little more level, I'd just as soon not landscape the side of a mountain today. This is eight seven will do. I've got you in sight be advised that is our team directly to your north and will pop a panel, let me know if you have us and remember, we have on black uniforms. Roger eight seven...you can move just east of your location about one hundred yards and we can effect a pick up, I'll keep you in sight. I've got two gun ships up here and will keep an eye on things till we get you guys out of there. Can we get the whole team on one chopper. This is eight seven—roger, one load will make it. Here they come. Get on. The door gunner I swear was trying to shoot me. Team on, lets get the hell out of here, they can pick up their own bodies (ten last count). Not a bad days work. Now lets get to the team house, give our report and have a drink. It was not going to be quite so easy this time. Our team commander's counterpart, Major Knock was getting more that just a little mad at how I was the one who (I'm sure) he was always trying to get killed and this lucky Irishman just managed to stay about five or ten bodies ahead of him...I should have shot that bastard when I had a chance. The son-of-a-bitch all but implied that I wasn't pulling off the operations as they were planned and discussed at the team house. No shit! The communist bastard was advising his relatives and friends, who were either V.C. or V.C. sympathizers. But that's another story and I did advise my team commander and was told they were already aware and were dealing with it, but to carry on the way I had been but be especially careful of my own counterpart and the road from the team house to my outpost. He said they were trying to get me. Hell, he implied that he do something about me or they would do something to him—fuck it! I guess in a way I don't blame him. He had been in country for two years and was getting tired of the bureaucracy as well.

Things were beginning to change. You could sense it. One day I saw something at the team house that no way in hell was I supposed to!! Money! Money, and large sums of it being delivered to the team house by an unmarked jeep, by a total stranger (to me). He looked American, but I found out he couldn't even speak English, I know, I listened!—he was German...what the hell is going on here! I know what I saw because they opened the brief case on the hood of the jeep—I know they had to see me, or were totally oblivious because of what was going down. I kept my mouth shut.

I had heard about Pro-American stations that were being set up using counterfeit American money, but we were an "A" site and not equipped to run psy-ops...that was a totally different unit within Special Forces. There was no way we could set up the type of operation and spread bogus money around the province trying to obtain information...there were to many individuals involved and they would all end up wanting a cut. This would have backfired and the people would have turned the tables on us and started selling info to the Viet-Cong. No! What I had seen was something I was not supposed to and the money, a lot of it, was not counterfeit!! I'm almost certain of it.

I finally figured out a part of the operation. There were a number of (F.A.C.) Forward Air Control Pilots who were showing up at the team at odd times under the guise they were selling Gold Rolex watches at a steal price when in effect they were only picking up the counterfeit money that was being delivered to certain areas in exchange for a watch or two and flying the money back to the base in Thailand where gold was purchased and sent back to the states. There were many people involved in high places to include high ranking Vietnamese Officers, some of whom repatriated to the U.S. after the war. Somehow I got the feeling that my life in the field was getting more difficult...more movement in my sector, heavy contact on night ambush sites, getting shot at by American choppers when we were returning from patrol in broad daylight—and it was only going to get worse!

CHAPTER TWO

Putting a Tuxedo on a Dinosaur

I have never understood why ancestry in our Irish clan was stressed almost to the breaking point. You are born, you live and you die… what happens in the middle is what we as individuals make of it. What happens in the end is, well….just that! You die. What always amused me is when some damn fool made a statement like "you know he was a drinker" or "he smoked all his life"…always some idiotic, inane statement that for some reason certain people feel must be said at a funeral—like my Dad. He was eighty five.

Just how long did they think he was going to live. Usually its some puritanical prick that croaks when he or she is fifty or sixty and everyone says—my-my they look so natural (in the casket). What did they die from? Being too good! Oh well, I'd like to hear what will be said at my repose.

I remember when I was a kid hearing the phrase "do you want to grow up and be like him"? Usually they were referring to someone in the family—their family, but they always made it sound like it was some person they happened to know who just got out of jail, was the local drunk or was unfortunately born with some defect that no one understood…thus setting that person aside from the mainstream to be the brunt of every joke or snide remark. Oh yes, and as I discovered as I was growing up….to reflect attention from the inbred morons in their own family.

It was impossible to do anything right when I was a kid…seemed like the only one who could get away with anything was the one who was the biggest outlaw, but his parents had money and no one would dare blame him for fear that the local banker might call a loan on some farm. It was the bankers son who was the real turd in our town. He was a liar, a thief and I think a little loose in the sneakers. He and my uncle would have gotten along just fine!! All of my friends were the *"our gang"* *type*…real rag-muffins.

Then we grow up. Where did all my friends go?

We go our separate ways….sometimes by choice, others by absolute necessity. Everyone was looking for summer jobs and unless you happened to know someone who owned a farm and needed help, prospects were fairly grim.

But something always managed to come along. My grandfather was an undertaker. When someone died he always called me to wash the hearse, set up the display room for caskets and on occasion assist in moving (other) things. No big deal, it just seemed like an awkward type of a job for a kid my age…but it paid well, and after a funeral no one would come near me for a month. Eventually I ended up working on a farm my last two years in high school. I lived there (room and board). The work was hard and the days were long, even during the school year. Didn't mind milking cows or tossing hay, but the damn pigs were just plain mean and they really stunk…I usually ended up head first in a feeding trough or the slop barrel. Most of all I missed my brothers and sisters while I was on the farm. They were all much younger. I would always stop by and visit them and they all wondered when I was coming home—little did any of us know at the time, but it would never be. At least not in the sense "I'm home", "done on the farm", "now what"? No. My next step would be in the military. I missed growing up with my family.

What the hell am I doing in this damn rice paddy…seems like forever since the shooting started. Danny just got shot and it's getting worse. Where the hell are the Gun Ships!!

All I know is I'll kill one of these pigs if I get bit one more time.

I know that in another year if all goes as planned I'll be finished with school and it's off to join the Navy.

There's always something to do on the farm. You cannot escape the heat in the summer or the cold in the winter. Seemed like the years were going to fast at times. I was beginning to wish I could stay right where I was—and never get any older, or have to change and accept the fact that I would soon be on my own far from the small town where I grew up. Seeing some of the world—after all that's what the Navy recruiter told my Dad—not me....my Dad! I only overheard it and was a little excited and scared at the same time.

In May of the following year I graduated and within hours I found myself outside the gates of hell...Great Lakes Navy Training Center. Scared shitless. I was handed over to the guard at the gate and as my Dad pulled out of sight the screaming began. If I had any sense I would have turned around and walked right back out the gate.

Between the fear of wondering if I would ever see my family again and the toad in the White Hat screaming at me I guess I did what anyone would have done....piss my pants, do five hundred push up's and follow the son-of-a-bitch with the thorn in his paw! By the time he finally got us to a place where we could sleep for the night and he finally shut his mouth, I was in a state of shock, where I would remain for the next 12 weeks. If he was looking for attention, the son-of-a-bitch succeeded.

By the time I finished Boot-Camp I was ready to get to the ship everyone was always talking about. Once again this was not to be...at least not for a while. I was assigned to the school command at Great Lakes Illinois where I would be going to "Machinist Mate" Training— whatever the hell that was!! They said I had an aptitude for it.

As I look back they always placed people in training where they had an opening and would tell the individual that this is what they had an aptitude for. Thank God someone didn't just drop out of flight training...they would have told me I had an aptitude for flying jets and it would have been off to wrecking planes for a while!!!

I was not in training command for long when I got a call one night informing me that my Mother had died. At seventeen and far from home and lonesome for my brothers and sisters this hit me especially hard.

I was sent home immediately and my father was informed by the department of the Navy that if I would be needed at home they would make arrangements for a hardship discharge. He told them no. I'm ever so grateful he did. I found out later that had I been granted a hardship discharge, within a year I probably would have been drafted into the Army anyway…in cases like this they usually give you twelve months to get your affairs in order then call you back, not always to the same service you were separated from. At the time it would have been the army. After returning to Great lakes I was not ready to return to training and the Navy school command recognized it.

I was processed immediately for assignment to a Destroyer on the West Coast and off I went—time to (really) grow up. U.S.S. Benner (DDR 807) (Tin Can). In dry dock! What a damn mess. I arrived on the day of my eighteenth birthday! When I checked in and went aboard, a review of my records revealed I could type…now I had an aptitude for being a Yeoman (Clerk) where I would spend the rest of my Navy Career. Like I said, I am glad someone didn't drop out of flight training while I was at Great Lakes Illinois.

What a shit house. I was beginning to think I was in the wrong Navy. It sure did not look anything like the posters. These guys were tramps!

Things would change however, but it would only take a short six months of living like a tramp and every day looking like my worse day on the farm except there were no pigs.

Bunkhouse eight seven, bunkhouse eight seven. This is bunkhouse eight seven go ahead over. Your friendly gunship service has arrived…whatdaya need over? We have one wounded American and would appreciate if you could haul him to the nearest field hospital. Mark the LZ and we'll drop straight in…roger that, first make a run at the trees just to the north of our location. We stopped taking fire about ten minutes ago and you should have a clean run at it. Will back the team up to the LZ just to the south…need to get this guy out! Roger that…get ready Danny here they come, it's going to be a short run can you make it? No sweat! All you boys coming out? No. We have to stay around till morning and clean this friggin mess up. O.K., you're on your own eight seven—good luck! Nice doing business with you boys, call anytime. Checked on Danny as soon as we got back in…he was in the team house sucking on a cold beer nursing a hole in his leg. All he said was "what the hell took you so long"!

Danny was good people, great big guy from Georgia with a heart to match. He liked the action, loved the team life style and was the last one in the world you would think could pull some shit on anyone. Well, while he was healing he was getting bored just sitting around. I approached Danny with a scheme. As it turned out we would have to involve a few others. The idea was to scare the shit out of the team sergeant…he was a jumpy bastard anyway and we figured it would not take much. It would all depend on some good acting. First the idea was to create a diversion in the bar area—a small argument. No fists, just words! The third man was the pivot—he had to threaten to kill me and them some shoving and yelling. He was to get a cross bow off the wall and on a given signal shoot at me down the short hall to the rooms. Then the screams…you hit him in the neck…get the Doc, he's bleeding bad. (this had all been pre-arranged). We cut a cross bow shaft in half, taped to ends to an arch made of wire and put it around my neck, and then the old stand by—catsup! And lots of it. You bet, it looked like a good shot to the aorta—blood all over the place. By the time the team sergeant got to me he was ready to faint (white as a sheet) and speaking in tongues. We thought the poor bastard was going to have a heart attack and had to blow our cover. He screamed for a week. Everyone headed out, I went back to the mountain and Danny was left, wounded leg and all to listen to the threats of revenge. All this was mild compared to some of the other shit we pulled.

I knew right then and there the Navy was not going to be the place for me…I did not however, feel that I would make such a rapid transition into the Army a few short years later.

By the time I had turned eighteen however, and whether I stayed in the Navy or not, it was time to grow up.

Most of the guys on the ship I was assigned to must have felt the same way….they all had that half scared look on their face, just left home and everyone they ever knew behind. Some were from the big cities, others, like myself were from small farm towns across the country and we all stuck out like sore thumbs and at the same time trying our best just to blend in. Easy for some, not so for everyone. Myself, I was still running on the same fear the guy at the gate in Great Lakes, Illinois put in me the first night I arrived for training.

"Join the Navy and see the World" my ass! I'd like to run into the guy who dreamed that one up! Probably some Army recruiter…but, it worked for me!!

I can't say that all my time in the Navy was a bad experience—it wasn't. Did manage to get to Hong Kong, Japan, Korea, the equator (shell back), Seattle Washington (sea fair), San Francisco and a few smaller cities on the west coast. What amazed me the most is the shear numbers of "Shore-Patrol" (Navy Cops) that were available in all of these places. Like one night in Yokuska Japan. Again, understand that I had not been in the Navy long at the time. I left the ship alone and headed down town for a little recreation. I got off the main drag and onto a back street and stumbled into a bar with nothing but beautiful women…things got really quiet. I thought I had died and gone to sailor heaven. Thank you St. Elmo. It was not long before I figured out why and was asked to leave in a not nice way. After collecting my thoughts and running like hell I realized that the place was for lesbians. I had no idea what that meant. I was just a young gullible country boy. Ran into the shore patrol coming out of the alley and bingo, got another free ride back to the ship. They explained it to me on the way back. The place was "off Limits"! What a waste. I never had to worry how I was going to get back to my ship…most of the time I got a free ride! God always had fun playing little tricks on me.

After a short while you begin to settle in and get a little more comfortable with your surroundings, all twelve square feet of it. Your rack (bed), canvas stretched on pipe with a thick hankie called a mattress. Home for the duration on the ship. I was used to small spaces like this. It's something you learn in the back seat of most older model cars, and a home that had more kids than square footage.

I remember the first time they passed the word to man the refueling stations. I knew where to go but I'll be damned if I had the slightest idea what the hell was going to happen. The seas were bad and water was coming over the rails…here we are trying to pull up along side this Carrier. I wondered just how they were going to pull this one off. All-of-a-sudden, Boom!

Some damn fool Bosin-Mate was standing next to me with what seemed to be a shotgun. I wondered who pissed him off.… I thought he shot at someone on the Carrier…it was a gun with a ball of string shoved in the barrell. First the small nylon cord and as soon as the Deck hands on the carrier grabbed that it was tied off and a larger line was tied to it and pulled over until finally the cable was drug out—rings and all attached. This is what they attached the fuel line to. As soon as it was over it was hooked up and the refueling began—holy shit what if this damn thing breaks? We were bobbing around like a cork. This took skill. The Captain was a real ass but he knew how to handle the ship in any situation. An hour later it was cast off and get the hell out of the area before we got sucked in to the blades of the carrier.

Was I scared? You bet your ass, but just like everyone else we went below and cleaned up and nothing was said except "it was a little rough out there" and then dead silence. The men on duty went to their stations and the rest tied themselves into their racks and slept it off.

I remember one time when we were pulling into Japan (Sasebo) and everyone was looking forward to a little time on the beach….beer, broads, and whatever else!! The one thing I do remember someone telling me is to stay away from the "Red Dot Akadama". A kind of Japanese wine made from God knows what…that it would drive a person absolutely nuts. That's one thing I should have not heard. I think I made it to about the second or third bar before I decided to try the damn stuff. Seemed harmless enough. The next thing I remember I was back on the ship, in the brig wondering what the hell happened. I was informed that I came back on my own volition and then all hell broke loose…someone told me to go below and hit the rack. I guess I thought this was some offensive remark and started to climb one of the mast and was going to dive over the side and go back to town. Then out of no where I spotted someone below me (I was on the 0-1 deck) it was obviously an officer and I decided to jump on his back…..BIG, BIG mistake! It was the Old Man, the captain. He was getting ready to leave the ship and I landed squarely on his back, proceeded to pull his hat down over his eyes and got captured.

Needless to say I spent the evening in the guest quarters, with bars. The next day was Captain's Mast, corporal punishment on the 0-1 deck. By this time everyone in the 7th fleet had heard what I had done and everyone in the squadron was watching to see what was going to take place. Most of them were betting I was going to be flogged. A hundred years earlier they would have hung me. What I got was a slap on the wrist. No one, especially me could figure out what had happened. The captain was known for his "hang-em-high" attitude and he let me skate. Gave me thirty days restriction (at sea). Where the hell did he think I was going to go. I guess the old man had a soft spot in his heart for dumb looking farm boys….or maybe he just saw something in me no one else did.

Neither of us realized it at the time, but our paths were somehow intertwined. We were on a short shakedown cruise and I had heard some of the officers talking about the "Old Man", the Captain, receiving orders for Vietnam—said something about the embassy!? It may as well have been in Chinese for all I knew, but was to find out a few short years and another branch of service later…we both were headed in the same direction.

When the time was getting close for me to get out of the Navy I had heard of a program that would get me out up to three months early to attend college. I had no idea what the hell I would do if I did manage to get into an institute of higher learning! What…expand on a dismal four years in high school!

With absolutely nothing to lose I gave it a try.

I put in for an early out for just this reason and they approved it! Who-da-thunk! There was a lots of space between me and the admissions office at the local college and it would only take seventeen years to get there.

CHAPTER THREE

Second chance in Hell

After pissing around at some meaningless job in California for a few months, and the laying of hands on one to many ladies, I decided to get back into the service. The Navy was out of the question. I thought about the Marines and decided on the Air Force. I had not even given the Army a thought. When I went to the recruiting office, all appropriate documents in hand, it was lunch time and the Air Force recruiter was not in. The Army recruiter was in his office next door and like a used car salesman he saw me lurking about and came over and introduced himself.

What a snake oil salesman this guy was.

We talked about what I was doing there and he started his fast sell. Five minutes into his ranting he asked if I would like to go and get a bite to eat and grab a beer....that's all she wrote! After half dozen brews he asked me if I had my separation papers from the Navy—which I did. He looked them over and said that I would not have to start over at the very bottom...damn close, but not the bottom. He felt after speaking with me I would be successful in Army intelligence....again, I'm glad someone didn't drop out of flight school that day because you can bet—well you get the idea. I was about to plug a hole in his quota for the month. The only thing this guy said that actually came true was that I did not have to go thru army basic training…all I had to do then was sign the papers and it was off to Fort Ord California where I was to be processed in and issued uniforms. On arrival I was placed in "prior Service" baracks with others who obviously had not had enough of civilian life, were drafted, or just to damn lazy to find a regular job. Myself and one other guy were the only ones from the Navy. There were air force, army and marines. We were told that we would be going thru basic again like it or not—but this was by the idiots we were bunking with. The day the orders came in and we ordered in to formation, two names were called out…mine and the other navy guy. Laughter was abound and when the Sergeant in charge heard this "he shit"! The two of us were given our orders to go to uniforms, get shots and sign out for our new assignments. The rest of the idiots were to recycle back thru basic. A lot to be said about pissing off the wrong person!

What a mess…didn't know how to put the uniform on properly, when or where to salute and still calling officers Mister. Some captain took me aside and recognized that I must have been prior Navy or Marines and gently corrected me. That means he did not chew my ass out or threaten to have me court-martialed for insubordination.

Holy shit! I'm on the damn ambush roster again. That means that Sergeant Coke lost another pair of glasses. I don't know if the rest of the team recognized that, (I'm sure they did), every time he came up on the roster he either broke his glasses or lost them. Hell, one time he was on the roster and when the word to "saddle up" (get ready to move out) was passed he actually made it to the truck. He even got on the back…then, as regular as any other time they fell off his face and when he got off to get them he stepped right on the lens. Oops! Well, he can't go out—again!! I just cannot figure to this day where he got all of the glasses he seemed to come up with the next day—he must have had a hundred pair of the damn things. Well Egan, it's your turn on the replacement…again! Nothing new. The only problem was that almost every time I went out we made contact with the local Viet Cong (V.C.). Sooner or later this shit is going to catch up with me and besides that I'm getting tired of going back thru the area the next morning cleaning up the bodies and trucking them to the river bank. After they were lain out, relatives and friends would pick them up and bury the bodys. I really never gave much thought that some of them may have families. If I allowed myself that, I would have started to make mistakes and that was unacceptable. I had people that worked for me that I had to worry about, and I knew most of them didn't have families, at least none I knew of. I was invited to the homes of many of them at one time or another— they called them cousins. Not once did I ever carry a weapon into one of their homes….and they respected that! That was the trust I had built up with the locals in my area.

Little did I know while I was attending Army Intelligence school that a few short years later I would end up in Fort Bragg, North Carolina attending "the John F. Kennedy Center for Special Warfare"….and home of the 18th Airborne Corps and the 82nd Airborne Division.

Let me set the records straight.

I was first assigned to the 11th Air Assault Division at Fort Benning, Georgia (which was later to become the 1st Air Cav. Division). Just before the division was to ship out for Vietnam I was reassigned to the 2nd Infantry Division at Fort Benning, Georgia. By this time I had met a girl from Florida one weekend while on a much needed rest from training and a few short months later we were married.

Janice (my wife) and I rented a very small trailer (mobile home) to live in…approximately eight feet wide by twelve feet long the kitchen table doubled as an ironing board the shower and toilet were one in the same and the kitchen sink looked like a Dixie cup, in a park you usually see depicted in horror movies. You know….the park manager with one tooth, bare footed, bald, in bib overalls with a vocabulary of about five words. The rest was grunts, nods and odd body movements. This bastard was frightening!!! I swear, if I had spotted a chain saw in the back of the dilapidated pick up truck he was driving, I would have grabbed Janice and ran.

This would also be a another first for the two of us. My wife understood this situation much better than I did. She came from a small town in the Florida panhandle that, for the most part was not much different than this trailer park and she enjoyed taking care of one of the small kids that seemed to always find his way to our door-step when they were hungry. One of the little tykes always had a baby bottle full of something. I thought at first it was a thick pablum but as it turned out it was curddled milk and that was just about all Janice could take.

By this time, Janice herself was about five months pregnant and was displaying all the instincts of a hibernating bear, and you had better, by God, not fool with her. She was pissed! Took the bottle, cleaned it, washed the kid, changed his diaper ordered me to the store to get milk and then fed the little shit, all while I was sitting very quietly in the corner observing, not daring to say a damn word...I just know she would have broken something on my body If I had.

I was assigned to the administrative unit of the 2nd Infantry Division Headquarters...I could type! Like I said I'm glad someone did not drop out of flight school. In the Military...no matter who you are, if the Military has a need for your service, you have an apptitude for it. You are committed for "X" time and they will use you as they damn well please....even if its only to bolster the Ego of some Idiot officer and believe me the Army was repleat with them.

Things have changed since then thank God!

There was this Red-Headed "Prick" Captain in charge of the unit I was assigned to. For some unknown reason he hated anyone who had prior service, especially in the Navy. I fell right in. No rhyme, no reason...he just hated me and I was about to incur his wrath.

Every shit detail he could think of.

I got to be friends with one of the guys there who lived in the same area I did off post. This shit-head captain, for some reason hated Mike about the same as me—only thing was, Mike understood the system one hell of a lot better than the idiot running the place. I think that was the problem, Mike was far smarter than he was and the damn fool knew it. Finally one day, Mike had just about all he could take and he knew I was about to blow a cork. He suggested that he and I put in a request to attend Jump school "Airborne" training right there at Fort Benning, Georgia. I'll never forget the day we dropped out requests' on the Captains desk....fire came from his nostrils! All he said was "if you two do not make it—do not come back here"! The only reason he approved our request is that he knew in his heart we would never make it and have to come back and face him.

Mike cautioned me that we had to toe-the-line for the next two weeks while waiting for assignment to jump school...this bastard was after both of us. That friggin Captain should have been tossed out of the service. Seriously!! I have a feeling he was called to active duty from some cushy job because of his reserve status. The troop build up in Vietnam was starting and he probably thought he would end up in a combat zone and was going to take it out on anyone he could.

He would have lasted about five minutes in country and someone would have popped his ass! If I ran into him now (today) I would crack his skull.

For the next two weeks Mike and I ran every chance we got, to somewhat get in shape for Airborne training. Then the big day…sign out for jump school. We signed in at school the same day and all hell broke loose and did not let for the next four weeks.

I asked Mike if he knew what he gotten us in to and what the hell would happen if we ever went back to the 2nd. I guess that was all the incentive either one of us needed. The next two weeks was all ground training. One of them was called "Hell Week". They should have called the whole damn thing "HELL SCHOOL"! There was no other way to describe it. Then the towers. Two hundred and fifty feet from the ground to the top. Yes, the next week was getting dropped off them in a pre- deployed chute. They would strap you in and haul you to the top. When the apex hit your ass slammed shut and away we went to the ground—day after day. Finally the big day came, we boarded the C-130 for the final time at Fort Benning, Georgia and about to land hanging under a parachute, in Alabama for the third and final time.

The only way out now was to get killed on the final (qualifying) jump.

We made it, and some Colonel was running to the drop site pinning wings on whoever he could reach on the drop zone. He was pinning on what everyone reverently referred to as our "Blood Wings"! I wasn't to sure what that meant, or what the hell he was doing, nor did I care. By the tone in his voice and the fact he shook our hands and saluted us with a hardy "congratulations", I knew we had made it! I was in a state of shock and about fifty yards away I saw Mike looking at the sky smiling like he just saw God! Now all we had to do was go back to the 2nd Infantry Division, pick up our orders, sign out and head for Fort Bragg, North Carolina.

We were both a little apprehensive about walking in the last day in the 2nd. Didn't know what to expect. It was like the inside of a tomb. Everyone was ordered not to speak to us. Our orders were tossed across the Captains desk, some of which fell on the floor. Right then and there I wanted to hit the son-of-a-bitch. Mike sensed it, jabbed me, and we both snapped to attention, saluted the prick and walked out. Signed out for the final time and left the building. This bastard knew Mike and I both had families and that my wife (Janice) was pregnant. He wanted us to cower and we refused…not overtly…it was like a chess game—one wrong move and its Check-Mate. But we won!!! Mike and I stopped in and had a beer on the way home and for about an hour all we could do was stare at ourselves in the mirror on the back bar of the dive we were in. This shit house was a real combat zone, not to far from our homes. Usually on weekends the cops were out at least ten times. It was "off limits" but we figured what the hell, one beer can't hurt.

Once again I find myself getting ready to head up a team of the finest outlaws in Vietnam…"my people", as I lovingly referred to them. Vietnamese, yards, cambodes and Nungs…who gives a shit? We all trusted one another and that is all that counted. No need for conversation, we knew the mission, we knew the target. Set up an ambush, wait and hopefully if contact was made, we killed them before they killed us.

Jump School!….a lifetime ago and a million miles away. Funny what you think about once you board the transport vehicle and everyone gets (real) quiet….knowing this might be the last time we see each other alive. Seems funny that we all spoke a different language and yet were all sitting there thinking the same thing. I wished a thousand times I had that prick Captain from the 2nd Infantry Division with me on one of these ambush'. He would have lasted about 30 seconds and then shit himself and I would have stood there smiling. This was going to be another one of the "not as usual nights". about half an hour after dusk one of my people saw movement on the edge of the rice paddy coming in from the mountains. Viet-Cong.. heading to the village to plunder whatever food he could and in the process rape one of the women or kids. Again, this was not to be. The cry went out- "V.C." and all hell broke loose. We took out the first man but little did we know that the main element had already made it to the village just prior to our arrival. Now we had to decide if we fired into the houses or sucked them out into the open…I chose the latter (damned if I know why), but it worked! The main element exposed themselves and headed back toward the mountains. We called for air support and light from spooky. The rest was history. Only four kills that night, but we went in early, only to have to come back the next day for body count and drag the remains to the riverbed where they would be claimed before sundown.

Ever wonder why you even get out of bed some mornings.

If I had it to do over again—from the gates at the Great Lakes Naval Training Center Illinois to the Army prior service barracks at

Fort Ord, California to jump school and everything in between—*"I'd do the same damn thing all over again"!*

Now all I have to do is fill out another after action report. Who initiated contact, where, how many? V.C., NVA.. All the usual shit, and the trick was to keep yourself as clean as possible, at all costs... they (V.C.) initiated contact. In my case I really didn't have to worry to much about it. The trigger happy loons that worked for me had big mouths...they ALWAYS yelled first, then shot, by that time we were always taking fire. *Kind of like when you were a kid and came home all beat to hell and had to explain some fight. The first thing out of my parents mouth was "who started it"?*

There were a few times when I got a little depressed. Not over the war, but leaving my family. I learned to shake it off. I knew if I had dwelled on it I would get myself and someone else killed. It didn't stop me from thinking about my wife and kid. I still remember her being nine months pregnant and under a doctors orders not to travel the day we left Fort Benning and headed to Fort Bragg. Joanie (our daughter) was born at Fort Bragg a few weeks after our arrival and things were really in a turmoil. Thanks to a couple of understanding N.C.O.'s in the 82nd I was given the time to get things squared away before getting settled in to Division activities...where I was assigned to the Division replacement outfit as a TAC NCO. Lousy hours, great people...and here-I-are! Still knowing precious little about the regular army and they assign me to the 82nd. The finest fighting men in the world, and one Dummy! Me! I almost forgot to mention (Mike). We both got assigned to the Div. Replacement. Mike and I were sidekicks. Thick and thin, good times and bad—we hung together, and thanks to Mike he further educated me on Army life. We had made it out of hell and were now, once again, looking to broaden our horizons! Mike didn't need a hobby, he had one—Me!

Holy shit, what next!?

Like I said, I knew very little about the regular Army...still in the Navy mode, or somewhere in between. One day when Mike and I were on our way home and I spotted a guy in a real weird looking uniform with a green thing on his head...I asked Mike what Army that guy was in. After his laughing calmed down he explained that he was a "Special Forces" type. I thought, what the hell was that? I made the mistake of asking Mike to explain…he must have thought I was kidding and maybe just testing him.

He said "are you for real"? You ever heard of the Green Berets? My answer—No!

About this time I think he was getting ready to dump me on the side of Bragg Boulevard…but I'm a fast learner and after some reading up and checking of my own I now felt I could approach Mike about this on a little different level. I let him think I was kidding!

It must have worked. Well, maybe. Mike was no fool.

About a month later he asked me if I would like to apply for Special forces training at the "John F. Kennedy Center for Special Warfare (special operations).

Sure, why not!

He told me he knew someone at the JFK Center and could help us out and that's just what we did, and in the process we pissed off another bunch of people. Shades of the 2nd Infantry Division! Seemed like every time we tried to better ourselves someone would treat us like outcasts. I finally figured out why. Not everyone who applied was accepted, and the ones that were stood a chance of not making it thru training, then it was back to where you came from and you can bet they would not be waiting with open arms. Once we put in our papers there would be no turning back and we had better finish what we started. I put my trust in Mike, he seemed to know someone just about every place we went and he knew Army reg's inside out…I looked up to the guy, but I thought to myself one day if Mike ever asks me if I want to try out one more thing I'm going to kill him. We got into more shit together than anyone I've ever known.

I finally figured out that there were two armies. One for the men who only wanted the best and would stop at nothing to get there…the other was for the low life bastards who were content to get spoon fed bull-shit, keep their mouths shut and when the time came, get out and crawl back to where they came from—leaving in their wake a trail of ruined careers. I often wished I had the Vaseline concession in a couple of these units! Ass kissin bastards!

CHAPTER FOUR

(Things are changing—and damn fast!)

Our time on the hill (82nd Airborne Division and Special Forces) was a memorable one—one I'll never forget, nor do I feel our wives will either.

Special Forces was one of the smallest units in the U.S. Army and had the highest divorce rate of all the other services combined. Special Forces took care to insure that we knew who our new family was, who came first and every married man who made the cut knew it. These ladies, our wives, watched as each and every one of us were changed into something they no longer understood—but that was then. No matter how long we lived, where we went or who we met along the way, our lives would never be the same again—we all knew and accepted it…the ones who made it all made the same choice.

We were now and forever bound together by a strong cord of conviction to one another and there is no room for outsiders. I was assigned to one team and Mike another and after that we kind of went different ways—only because of our team and training status. One day Mike came by and informed me he was headed for Nam (Vietnam). I began to wonder what I should do next, but I knew in my heart what I had to do. Special Forces Soldiers were also known as triple volunteers; jump school, Special Forces Training and Vietnam. We ALL volunteered.

By this time, my brother Jim who had been living with us for about a year, quit school and took off (he was seventeen). He headed back to Wisconsin and conned Dad into signing the papers so he could join the Marines...the next thing I know he's graduated from boot camp and headed for Vietnam—it was just that fast! I went to see the Team Sergeant and advised him I wanted to head for Nam...O.K.! No pomp—just OK! Fill out your request and I'll sign it...that's just the way things worked. At that time things were getting bad in country and they were looking for all the replacements they could get. Most of our teams were getting hit pretty hard and the casualties were mounting faster than anyone wanted to talk about. There was always the feeling that you were saying goodbye to everyone you knew for the last time. You signed out and left quietly.

Jimmy was already in country and his unit was getting their ass kicked on a daily basis...I figured I'd never see him alive again either. The last word I received regarding him was that his unit was trapped in the Khe Shan Valley and that he had been shot.

We both accepted our fate.

We had another brother in country...he was in the air force. He was in Saigon at the Ton-sa-nuht (sp) air base. I did have to go to Saigon one time to identify a body and while I was there I stopped by the air base to visit him...barracks, air conditioned, clean sheets on Beds! Lockers! Holy shit, what war are these guys in? Well, not quite that nice, but a bed of nails would have been comfortable for me. I must have looked pretty strange to his friends—Dirty, five different weapons, three of which I was using for trading material—food mostly.

The Air Force was notorious for great food and I was not leaving without a case of steaks. Thru neglect or design I did not spend much time with brother John...He thought (knew) I was on a mission to steal food, jeeps, etc., and get the hell back where I came from. I just know he did not want any part of my possibly getting caught and I didn't blame him. He had his hands full just trying to stay alive on that damn Air Base that seemed like it was getting mortared every half hour. I don't know how John put up with some of the people I met there... he had to work with them. They were all scared shitless and I never saw any of them carry weapons and from what I saw it was probably a good thing—some of them would have given the phrase "friendly Fire" a brand new meaning. I knew I had to get back up north so I located

John and asked him if he could get me a ride back up north. I figured he must know someone, he had been there two years. He said I couldn't get out for two days and the only thing leaving then was a plane called the "Black Bird" (highly classified) and no one could get on it. John didn't know it at the time but others in our unit used it all the time. I left that day and headed back to my team. Never saw John in country again...he was due to rotate shortly after I left and go home. Saigon would be safe another day—they separated the Egan brothers!!!

It was good getting back to the team.

What are you doing here Egan? Get kicked off the mountain. No, had ambush last night. Going to clean up and head out...after I drink this place dry—wise ass! Have a tough night in the team house Coke? See ya found another pair of glasses. How many of those fuckers you go anyway. None of your damn business. I see you're on the roster for tonight! I thought the poor bastard was going to break his neck getting to the Bulletin Board. Once again, he turned and said "kiss my ass you smart fuck"! He wasn't there, but it was fun shakin his cage....as a matter of fact the team commander told me to stop picking on him, he hasn't got that much time left in country and when it comes time for him to go I want to make sure he can find the door.

Now would be a good time to go back to my outpost on the mountain...I stirred up all the shit I could for one day. Besides that I kind of liked being aound people who just accepted you for what you were and respected their way of life rather than trying to shove some American bullshit down their throat. I led them to believe my life was not much different here than it was at home and the only way out for them was to fight.... sounded more like a coach trying to rally a losing fooball team at half time. I would always carry my PEN Double EE (camera) with me and when I was in the village surrounding my camp I would try and get pic's of any known or suspected V.C. sympathizers...being careful not to be noticed. That would have destroyed my credibility...trust was a big issue with the Vietnamese—you earned it. Keeping it was like tap dancing on the edge of a razor blade. I never did trust the (Vietnamese) warrant officer who was my counter-part. You really did not have to be trained in counter intelligence to know this bastard was always up to something...he asked way to many questions about the types of operations they launched from our base camp and when I told him I did not know he would get pissed, walk off for a couple of hours and always come back—never apologize, but rather say he had a bad night or some other bull shit. He was way to quick with the rhetoric. I reported him several times to the team commander, who in turn reported to his counter part (Major Knock). This would always lead to accusations that I was trying to get him and Mr. Dhang (my counterpart) killed or at the very least replaced. Nothing could have been further from my mind...I wanted to see both the bastards caught. The Vietnamese Warrant Officer at Camp Sui Dau was another one who I never trusted from the first time I every spent the night at that desolate hole in the road they referred to as the A-502 "model outpost" and as I was about to find out a few shorts months later, they should have paid more attention to security than pretty!! It was no more than a rest stop during the day for NVA regulars and V.C.. There were no Americans in the Camp during the day and any of the regulars that worked for us who opened their mouth would be discounted and shot...the report would later read that they had simply deserted. I always wondered if the nights I spent there would somehow be by last...maybe I just did not want to believe what I had suspected for a long time was true.

Night after night you get your team ready to leave the relative safety of the outpost and head for the rice paddys. You radio your tentative coordinates to the base camp so they can mark it on the board just in case you get hit and need Spooky, the gun ships or a dust off. This is one area you did not deviate to much from your planned ambush site. There were many, many choppers in and out of the area and they had the same orders we had...anything spotted after dark was fair game, and that included us. Guerilla warfare and counterinsurgency is all it's cracked up to be, it is also very dangerous. Didn't make much sense to me when I found out who was always hanging around the radio room (Major Knock) so I would always move just outside the area I reported I would set up our ambush site. Our only salvation was calling in first in case of contact with the V.C. and let them know we would mark our location with a strobe then hope and pray some trigger happy asshole door gunner didn't spot us before the pilot called him off...all in all they were pretty good. Once we called them in and gave them a fire mission and they were advised it was Special Forces they knew how we dressed (just like the V.C.) and were extremely careful to lay down fire exactly where it was directed and would come up on the frequency given and be in contact with the man on the ground as soon as possible. Spooky was always my favorite...all the light we needed and it usually sent Charlie on the run, and along with that, 20MM cannons that would turn five thousand feet of concertina wire into mill end metal shavings in thirty seconds flat. The accuracy of which they could put forty thousand rounds in an area the size of a card table in about thirty seconds. What we didn't kill the gun ships would.

The team commander approached me in the team house on one of my scavenger runs one day and told me that I could take a few days down time if I wanted.

Funny part was this was only two days after I spotted the funny black jeep and the occupants who had German sounding voice' and a brief case full of money. The one that was dressed like one of us but with absolutely no markings just like his vehicle. When he left the case was not with him and he stayed about two minutes!!! What the hell was going on around here? None of my business and I kept it that way—at least for a while.

I never let go of that Nagy little situation and would later find out what it was all about—and for my own safety, once again, I kept my mouth shut! After handing me a hundred bucks out of what the team commander said was the team fund, I asked where the hell I would go—he said anyplace in country…maybe he thought I would take my team and start another war someplace else and he would no longer have to contend with my bullshit. He loved it, but he was running short of excuses trying to explain to the shirts in Nha Trang why, every time I came in…for any reason…Group Headquarters motor pool would shrink by one more jeep. It beat the hell out of walking forty five clicks back to the team house before dark.

I would spend most of my time in the club…quietly, just watching. Ocassionally I would roam around the base compound and watch the pansy asses in pressed uniforms and clean boots. Once in a while you run into someone you knew from one of the other teams—in Nha Trang for the same reason I was. Lift what you could (booze) (food), put it in a hot jeep and get the hell out of Dodge. If you saw three guys from (I) or (II) corps you can bet there would be four less jeeps in the motor pool some time in the next few hours. They couldn't say a hell of a lot—most of the equipment there was stolen from some leg outfit and repatriated to S.F.. Seemed like everyone there was running around in new looking jeeps and it pissed them off when they got outwitted.

Egan, you going out tonight? There's a couple of strap hangers (out-siders who wanted to go along for the ride and hopefully see some real combat). Damn, I didn't like taking them along…made my people uneasy. Made me uneasy. We knew each others moves and if you plug a stranger in they just got in everyones way and it made my people uneasy They always seemed to show up in pressed uniform…steel pot…carbine…nine thousand rounds of ammo…a flak-jacket…canteen…big knife and anything else they could carry without resorting to a fork lift to board the transport vehicle. They would shit when you told them to get all that shit off…give them an M- 16, six mags, a soft hat and a canteen of water and said that's it! Don't worry—if we get hit and we haven't ended things before running out ammo we would be in deep shit and have to run anyway. No need to carry more than we had to and it was every man for himself. Some of them actually said "no thanks"! Others had the balls to say that they were told to wear the junk at all cost—it was like they came along for a free ride and were going to dictate policy. All they really wanted was to get fired on and get included in an after action report so they would possibly be eligible for a "Combat Infantry Badge"—period! we actually had three marines show up one time—said they were going out with us and were going to wear what they damn well pleased! The team commander told them they would stay in the team house for the night and get the hell out in the morning. No one, but no one was going to march in and start dictating policy to his people. These people always seemed to show up ten minutes before it was time to head out to some ambush site so if you were going to take anyone along there was no time for argument. It was "do as I say" or do it someplace else.

I went to the team commander one time and told him I had heard that someone from 5th group headquarters was sending these bastards out. As it turned out, I was right. One of the Later Day Sergeant Majors at group was more of a politician than he was anything…a real ass kisser and would do anything he could to appease anyone who had more power than he did. Consequently we ended up with the half breeds that were related to someone in Washington and wanted their half wit son or nephew to be able to (ultimately) say he operated with Special Forces. Their real jobs were clerks for the most part…no balls and no brains! This same Sergeant Major also had a side business selling Rolex watches…what the hell has expensive watches got to do with anything…especially in the middle of a damn war…excuse me, Police Action!! This is the same guy that came out to visit our team and while there we were informed that all the skulls on the back bar had to be removed and buried. This guy was an ass hole—but he had power—of some kind, or over someone. Too much going on in this guys life and as he would eventually find out he should never have screwed with our team…it took some months but he finally got nailed. Phony medals, bogus money transfers, washing more money than he made from local and military script to green backs (American money), and that was only the tip of things to come. He was aiding in moving sums of money. I never in my life forgot anyone who tried to shit on me and always made it my sole mission to get even whenever possible. There is an old saying: "My enemies are all around me and my friends are mixed in there someplace".

People think that wars are just that…wars. Two sides shooting at each other…and the killing goes without saying, but after all who gives a damn. People in power on both sides all looking for the blue ribbon—at all costs.

There have been wars on this planet as long as there have been human beings and as the eons passed the wars only seemed to have refined themselves in weaponry. Men trained and skills honed. All for one purpose—winning! At all cost!

Along the way the battle field became an area where surgical life saving methods were developed, and as well medicines and communications devices. Items that were previously developed in a war zone are now in practical use in our everyday way of life….chief among them communications devices. Prosthetics is another area were the American soldier came into play. The many types of replacement units for arms and legs, plastic surgery for rebuilding faces and badly burned and scared bodies of our young men and women…all are a result of war and put into practical use by civilians only after they are tried and tested by our soldiers.

You do not think of this type of stuff when you are on some outpost in the middle of the jungle. You think about where the next bullet may come from and who it will find. He does not care about the politics…only staying alive, in hopes of one day returning home, back to a place that as a kid he was safe. A place where the only fights were between the brothers and sisters in the family. I think that our father would have preferred a war zone to the seemingly endless battles that went on in our loving family. We never think just how much fun it is until there is no longer anyone to pick at.

For Christ's sakes Herbie look what's coming up the hill—V.C.! Looks like a parade! Are they blind? They are walking right in to the compound. We are in deep shit! We gave the alarm and the team manned the gun posts and were given the command not to fire. They had their hands up! I thought I was dreaming—it had to be some sort of a trap, no way in hell were an entire company of Viet Cong going to walk in a surrender. They all had their hands up and the only weapons we could see were farming tools. Rakes, side cutters, hand made long knives—the works! But it was true. We disarmed all of them and for the next hour questioned and fed them... seemed like the only thing we could do—after all, if there was a reinforced company or worse an entire battalion of North Vietnamese regulars coming up behind them—I wanted to be as friendly as possible. By this time Herbie was getting friendly with all of the seeming leaders and from what he could gather they were just farmers before they were kidnapped and forced into battle with the Viet-Cong. That's the way things went—either the men cooperated or their families were slaughtered. This time, they had the only chance they thought they would ever have and escaped and were now wanting help for themselves and others who wanted to come in but were afraid. We had already radioed the base and informed them of what was transpiring. Before we could fart here they came, The S-2 (intelligence) officer—whom by the way (never) left the compound for an ambush like the rest of us and was afraid to visit the other outposts—what this bastard did was beyond me, but this time he saw an opportunity to really bask in the glory! On his and others arrival, Herbie and I were shunted off and told to return to base and to keep our mouths shut... the next thing I know this incident was being reported by all the major networks in the U.S.. I guess it was this little prick's last chance to bask in glory and he was not going to miss a drop. Anyway Herbie and I hit the bar as soon as we got back to base camp and sucked up all the free booze we could whilst the rest were out with the cameras, etc.. Oh well, just another day at work... it always made me warm and tingly inside when I could help the stars shine. What really bothered me that particular day was when I was told to leave (Herbie and I) and all my people were left in the camp wondering what to do... Viet-Cong prisoners on one side of the camp and a whole shit load of Audie Murphy's on the other side. To this day I wish they had just walked out of the camp, left the hill and went home.

CHAPTER FIVE

Tween Sailor and Suicide!

Somewhere between the Navy and the Army I did manage to have somewhat of a social life which was beginning to wear me out (physically).

I was renting a room in a house in the suburbs (someplace, California). At the time I got out of the Navy I was going with a gal who informed me of this place and I grabbed it.

Needless to say it would be real close to (female) companionship.

On occasion I would get a little closer than I should have. It was easy to pull it off with my girl friend, even with her parents around, however, on the other side of my house was a good looking young gal, albeit married who was beginning to show me more attention than the other liked.

At the time I really had no idea of the inherent dangers of even looking at a young married female let alone entertain the idea of.... Well, you get the idea. Now I was working day and night and weekends and it was beginning to take its toll.

It was either find a new diet or a new place to live—I opted for the later and joined the army where it was (a lot) safer and not nearly as physically strenuous. Funny what a person thinks about when he's alone in his mind. I could keep my mouth shut and enjoy myself briefly, even if at times I was waiting for the shit to hit the fan. Again and again I thought about my brother Jimmy. I had heard he got shot at Khe San. I had no idea what shape he was in.

This poor bastard had seen enough in his short life for ten people.

He was always a proud individual and when he researched the Marines I guess he decided they met his expectations—left home and hit the Boot Camp trail. When I heard about Khe San he was already back in the Ashau (sp) valley, once again getting his young ass shot off.

Once again, all the Kodak camera heads were on their way west on choppers ready to bolster their careers and I have no doubts that medals of "all sorts" got pinned on brass laden shirts that day...after all, it did end up on network television back in the states, but not until each and everyone of those bastards rotated and they were damn good and sure Herbie and I were out of the picture. Oh, what the hell!

I always wished Jimmy had joined the Army and gotten into Special Forces like myself. The Marines gain was our loss. He was the quiet unassuming type of person, just don't piss him off. He left the Marines after a four year stint and not unlike most he took up drinking as a hobby. After sobering up and attending college for a while he settled down in Las Vegas where he remains to this day.

There were to be other situations I would find myself in. I never had to wait long or go to far. Fortunately for me the "White Banshee" was Omni present. I have often wondered, if thru her screams, she managed to turn away some of the bullets intended for me.

You do not have to be Irish to understand the tale of the "white banshee" only pray the "Black one" neer finds yer trail.

As I said, I never had to wait to long.

A few days later the team commander asked me if I would take a team west of the base camp for a couple of days as there had been reports that since the Viet Cong defectors had come in there was beginning to be more and more movement reported in somewhat the same area—if not in the same direction. Coordinates and or exact locations were never obtained from the bunch that came in, only that the activity was increasing and in our direction and that meant North Vietnamese Regulars.

For the most part any patrols that were occasionally conducted during fly-over by choppers out of Nha Trang never managed to sight anything...which is not surprising given that most movement was at night. I was informed also, that the V.C. were coming thru the huge "rubber plantation" located in the area of my outpost and were dumping the bowls on the trees. This was life blood for the villagers who collected and sold this product which was used for a variety of reasons... none of which I was aware of, but they needed the money to live on. The north was moving south little by little and the sad part was they were killing their own people on the way especially any of whom were suspected of aiding the Americans in any way.

It was now getting personal.

One of the new guys assigned to the team (medic) asked if he could go along as he wanted to get his feet wet before settling in to a long grind as one of the team Doc's. These guys trained long and hard at Bragg and were saints on the team, a totally different breed...kind of like a real bastard among a bunch of just everyday bastards. Why not! I told the team commander and he agreed. I was briefed on the mission and went over the details with the Doc. Got the team together and told them we would be out for a couple of days and to pack accordingly. Gave them the game plan and when we saddled up to head for the drop off point, I gave them phony info...even the Doc recognized something was amiss but only questioned it after we were on station for the night.

I filled him in on the team commanders counter-part, the one who I had suspected for a long time wanted me dead. I did not dare to say anything prior to departure. Somehow the word always got out. Fuck, I hoped nothing went wrong now...I was the only one who knew where we were and I was not sure, but I knew that we would be alright for the night unless someone stumbled over us.

I had to break silence the next morning and inform base of our new coordinates and hope for the best...hope that the prick Vietnamese Major did not get wind of what was going on.

We made a sweep of the rubber plantation and it was obvious what they were doing. There was no indication of recent activity so my plan was to move to the north in an area I suspected they might be coming in from and set up for the night in hopes of hitting them in an ambush.

Things were quiet, all night. Almost to quiet and I was beginning to suspect that Major Knock found out and just did not know where we were. I feel certain that we would have been hit but he was now afraid to ask and if anything were to happen it would not look good for him!

The next morning we were getting ready to pack up and return to base and had only walked about one or two clicks east when all hell broke loose.

We were getting fired on by American choppers—I tried everything I knew to call them off, smoke (all colors) panels, radio. All to no avail. The medic was running all over the place…half the team shot up and when I saw the damn thing making a run at me I dove head first into a well on the edge of the village we had just came thru. By this time I was getting radio from base and they told me that the choppers had spotted V.C. in the area and were firing on them—it was us!! We dressed for the occasion, but this is one time when I "Did" let them know where I was…break contact, break contact!! Somehow, in the short period of time after we radioed in that bastard Major got wind to the Americans that a V.C. patrol was heading east and to fire on it.

Now I knew for sure that the major had something to do with trying to get me killed.

He was ready to sacrifice anything to get to me. That God damn Asian "lose face" "save face" horseshit had gone far enough! Now, half the team dead and one of the best Vietnamese troops that ever worked for us was laying there with his lower jaw shot completely off. I was beginning to develop a sense of how this was all going down. When I managed to get some straight answers over the radio base was told by the choppers they were being fired on and only returned fire—bull shit! And I did not pull any punches when the team commander came out to the location of the incident…once again, this incident was covered up and I was asked not to say anything.

I was told to inform the Doc.

I knew the Doc would go along, he was new on the team and had no intentions of making waves. No harm no foul. Now all we had to do was keep an eye on our own backs for while as we lost the respect and trust of what was left of the (Vietnamese) team.

For my own safety I never operated with them again.

I asked the team commander if I could meet with him (anywhere but in the camp). He agreed. The following week he called me on the radio and asked if I would come down off the mountain and escort him to Nha Trang. He needed a body guard. It did not seem unusual so no one suspected what it was all about.

When we arrived at 5th group headquarters he said let's go to the G-2 and kick this around. I said I'd rather not and asked him to just keep my suspicions between he and I for the time being. He knew in his heart what it was about and let me vent my feelings and why I felt the way I did…I hesitated to say that I felt Knock was using one of the team officers to gather intelligence, and it was not the team commander. The worse part is I suspected that the American officer knew and he had a bigger hard on for me than Major Knock. The two of them were buddies and I was not sure just how far reaching all this was at the time.

They both hoped and prayed I would meet my end sooner than later. Our team G-2 was not particularly fond of me. After a couple of months on the team and never really knowing who this fuck was…I only had seen him lurking about, I asked him one day who he was and what he did.

I was informed it was none of my business. Bad thing to say to a person who doesn't trust you to begin with—let the games begin!

I said I only wondered because I had never seen him do anything and knew for sure he had never been on the ambush roster. You could see the smoke and fire coming out of his nose.

I had seen him collecting many, many pictures of various operations that were pulled off and that he had a penchant for collecting and saving for (personal) use the souvenirs' taken off dead bodies—belt buckles, hats, patches, etc., all under the guise of needing them for information on units they were assigned to, their rank, and names if any so he could render them to 5th group. Seemed plausible so I let it go until I found out from a friend of mine he never said anything about this type of stuff in any of his reports to 5th Group G-2 in Nha Trang. He was mailing this stuff to himself in the states…war stories and all. Further, I managed to find out that he was more than just friends with the team commanders counterpart (Major Knock)

but was assuring him that he would sponsor him to come to the states after the war and help set him up in business. And you wonder where the money was going!!!!

Is it any wonder they both wanted me out of the way. Now I had to do all I could to protect myself and I began keeping a journal of activities. Mostly just planted bullshit I knew they both had access to and document what would transpire as a result.

No way in hell was I going to implicate any Americans in Knock's business, as I firmly believed he was being used and very artfully. I never said Knock was stupid.

The ultimate end for me seemed just around the corner at this point and I was getting more than just a little paranoid. What the fuck was that Major (knock) going to try next and just how had he managed to get so close this time. He knew! I didn't care, I was in so deep now there was no turning back. There was actually a time when I had wondered if I was already dead and God was playing tricks on me. This was probably the first time during my that I thought of God! I sure didn't blame him for anything and I did not ask for forgiveness and I didn't want to waste his time asking him to make some sense out of all this…maybe I really was dead and he just sent me back to figure it out on my own.

I returned to base and asked the Doc if he would look after what was left of the team. Patch them up as best he could and try to build some type of trust and rapport and maybe, just maybe he would be able to build them back to the fighters they were before that ill fated morning.

All I wanted to do is return to Nui Thi…I felt bad, I felt remorse I had not experienced before, I just wanted to be alone for a while. I knew I could always run back to the mountain—my safe place—kind of like the tree house you hid out in as a kid when you were in trouble or just needed to be alone where you could create an imaginary world where everything was nice—safe; free from conscience, worry, strife, hunger. Just safe even if only for a few fleeting moments.

By the time I returned everyone had heard of what happened. I was raked over the coals by my (Vietnamese) counter-part.

He was obviously going to make an effort to shame me for something I had no part in. He came as close that day to getting shot right between the eyes as he ever had that day.

I hated that son-of-a-bitch and there was now a brand new (personal) war about to erupt. I could sense it in his voice and I could also see the fear on the faces of my people on the hill.

They were afraid to stay around Mr. Dang (my counterpart) when I was not there and also afraid to say anything in my defense for fear of getting killed by the crazy bastard. I could not blame them, but I now had to do something before all was lost...I knew he was a V.C. Sympathizer, I just could not prove it. He was also one of Major Knocks henchmen and was keeping him informed of my movements.

From that day (night) on, I never slept in my bunker—I would move around at night when Dang went inside and move again if I sensed he had eyes elsewhere in the camp. I knew it was over and made contact with The team commander, He advised that I take some time and maybe head for Nha Trang or even Saigon for a while.

Special Forces had a safe house in Saigon so that was not out of the question—I needed time to think.

This was bad and I knew it.

I really had no idea what may be in store for me when I returned to the team but I had complete confidence in the Team Commander. Our team put that poor bastard thru hell. What of the chopper pilots that were in the air that day...they were some of the same guys that flew our area a thousand times and probably knew the terrain better than we did.

Someone put them in our vicinity at that moment. If it was an American, he was duped.

It was not usual to see these guys during the day unless there was need for an extraction. Air support was always needed at night. There was just no reason for them to be there. Who was really after my ass and why? Was it Knock? Was it something a little more sinister? My getting killed would have been a real convenience for several people. It had to look like line of duty. Anything less would have raised to many questions.

Maybe someone would have to answer for what I had witnessed at the jeep that day and they feared I might say something. Between that and Major Knock's face saving bullshit!

There was more to it.

There were more people at higher levels involved and like I said before, I had no desire (at that time) to dig into it. Hopefully I would be able to make it thru my tour alive—and now I did not even know who the real enemy was, but I was about to make it my life's work to find out!

CHAPTER SIX

(Back to work—checking my back)

After returning from Saigon where I eventually ended up, I checked in with the team commander. He asked if I was ready to go back to work and apologized for what happened. Hell, it wasn't his fault. I just know he was not involved in any way in things that were happening to me. It's a feeling I had and believe me my hunches kept me alive on more than one occasion. I'll figure it out.

I spent the night in the base camp team house. I did not sleep in the room that was usually assigned to me.

The next day I went to my interpreters house in the village. He usually stayed with his sister and brother in law when I was not around and he did not like operating with other teams. His people knew me. It was always fun to see the kids. They never said a word. They just smiled and would always lead me to a place to sit and then just stand and stare and smile. There was plenty of tea and always a bowl of rice.

The kids made me feel welcome and for a brief time I could just forget the war. If I ever asked God for any favors it was that he keep an eye on this family.

Later on that day I returned to the team house and checked the roster. I was not on it. I do not recall who was assigned the ambush for that night. Funny thing, it was not Coke! He was however assigned to make the trip to Sui Dau that night. All he had to do was get in a jeep, drive the short distance to the outpost, check in with the Vietnamese warrant officer that was assigned to the place, check the field of fire, claymores, etc., and bed down for the night.

I could not help but wonder how he was going to get out of going, but I knew somehow he would.

I ran into Sergeant Brown who I had seen around the team house on several occasions. I figured he was assigned to he team and just stayed to himself—kind of like me. Brown was a funny guy. Big smile, short hair and always a good joke. We had a beer and shortly thereafter the team commander asked if I would like to go to Sui Dau with Coke for the night. Brown, realizing that would probably not be a good idea volunteered to replace Coke and once again the world was a better place.

It was getting late and Brown suggested if we were going, now would be a good time to make the trip. You did not want to be on that road when the sun was going down free game and we both knew it. Saddle up, look back long enough to see Coke with his usual smug ass grin and hit the trail. I actually think I saw a tear in his eye.

We actually made good time, and half a mile from the O.P. Brown suggested we stop at a local roadside inn and have a beer. The camp was in sight so we felt confident there would be no problems.

The skies were eerily quiet. No choppers that are usually buzzing in the vicinity. Spooky not yet on station…almost too quiet on the way down.

It seemed that the closer we got the din of aircraft were beginning to fill the air. Everybody getting ready to go to work.

This is one time I hoped they all had the location of the teams.

I had no doubt that the air support units had the locations of all of our outposts clearly defined on the manning boards in their briefing rooms. I knew that the people (Vietnamese) that were assigned to Soui Dau had already heard of the team that got shot up and probably knew who I was and for this reason I was ready for a fairly chilly reception.

I knew that my personal location for the night was clearly marked at the team house. The one time Major Knock would have no trouble in locating me and letting particular individuals know.

I was more than just a little worried but never said anything to Brown. I don't think Brown cared much anyway. He was one of the best, always knew what to do, where to go and when to back off. We were on our way to this desolate, very vulnerable shit house and Brown had not blinked an eye. He knew about the team getting shot up and he knew my reputation. He never said a word. We kicked around our rotation date and both knew that this might well be our last assignment at least on the manning board! If we wanted, all we had to do was ask the team commander to pull us from normal operations.

Usually the last thirty days in country was spent in the team house and we only went out if someone on the roster got sick, injured (lost their glasses) or by our own request.

I wondered to myself what was going to happen to my outpost and the people in the village when I left. And what about my interpreter and his family? You know in your heart you will never see them again even if you come back.

You are usually assigned elsewhere on the return trip and there were several options open for guys on their second or third trip back. I had always wanted to get into (B-50) Omega. They were a strange bunch and somewhat selective, (invitation only) and you had to know someone.

I also thought about getting into SOG (Special Operations). Again, selective, not elective—invitation only! Second trip to the rodeo a minimum—and it also helped to know someone. These are all units within units, "enigmas" that operated in a highly clandestine fashion. Which simply put meant they could do as they damn well pleased whenever they felt like it, and answered to no one. Their locations were known but the areas they operated in were strongly guarded. We all knew this but never asked questions. So maybe, just maybe this would be in the offing. I would have to speak with some (other) people that I worked for if I returned.

From the time I joined the Army and my initial assignment at the Army intelligence school my movements were fairly well orchestrated and my assignments thereafter as well. The reasons always came later...and I had better keep my mouth shut!

Brown said maybe we have time for one more beer before we head out. The camp is in sight and there is still enough light.

Sure, why not I said to Ed. He said great, this one's on you! It took about two seconds to figure out I had just been hosed.

It was worth it to see the grin on Brown's face. I still had this feeling that this was different somehow. Different in the sense that it was unlike other trips I had made to this same place. I could not figure it out—just a gut feeling…I did mention it to Ed and all he did was roll his eyes, like he felt the same way but didn't want to say anything, not in the roadside bar. The lady who ran the place sold intel to the highest bidder—side be damned!

It was getting a little darker outside and we decided it was time to head out.

It was a quiet ride the rest of the way in. The area around us and the road to the camp was quiet…maybe to quiet! There is usually someone on a bicycle or a moped going home this time of night. Things were almost tranquil and the two of us decided to make the best of our little camp out.

By the looks of things just to the northeast of us someone had run into some kind of trouble. There were choppers heading out in that direction and it looked like spooky had come on station and went to work a little early. The quiet ride was over and Charlie was moving. Ed made some comment about who it might be as we had only one camp out that way, just not that far. We discounted it was any of the S.F. units.

We had passed some engineering outfit on the way down and it looked like business as usual there and we were hoping all would be the same for us. After we arrived at the camp and made contact with the Vietnamese Warrant Officer in charge when there were no Americans on site. There was the usual hand shake and the bowing. This is one of the other (VN) pricks I did not care for. He was always bragging about his martial arts prowess and was forever wanting to butt heads (literally) just to see how hard he could hit someone—I guess without knocking himself out. The first time he had tried this with me, it was my first visit to the place and was advised to go along with his antics. I thought what the hell…let him go to it. He took me by the ears and showed me what to do. The next thing I knew he was on one knee and trying to regain some composure. I knocked the bastard senseless! Didn't do myself any good either, but I stayed on my feet.

I was supposed to let him win. Someone should have told me. He was pissed and once again I had succeeded in one more of the bastards losing face.

There was a cold reception and I asked if he would like to get even…it seemed to really piss him off and he walked away.

Ed questioned what that was all about. After I explained he just grinned and shrugged his shoulders. I really had not put it all together until after the incident with Major Knock, and Mr. Dang, my counterpart. Now I had the three top Vietnamese officers assigned to our camp pissed at me and now wanting revenge. I knew he was probably aligned with the Viet Cong and I had made mention of that to our team commander. He only laughed and said everyone knew that. What the hell is going on here? I guess they figured the only way to get Intel on the activities in the area was to keep an eye on the people holding the reins.

It still seemed to me more than just a military relationship between our G-2 and the top Vietnamese Officer in our base camp. Didn't anyone care and what was that damn money was for I had seen that day by the jeep?

Once all the formalities were over Ed suggested we check the camp. All seemed in order until we got back in our bunker and Ed said that things just appeared to be to neat.

I made mention of the guards who appeared to be new and their uniforms which also seemed too new and clean to be assigned to this shit house. You have to be alert to subtle changes. The North Vietnamese and the Viet Cong were well adept at maneuvering into places like this and the one big thing they had on their side was fear. We had not realized it just then but almost everyone in the camp was new except for that damn Warrant officer. The ones we knew from previous stays there were trying to tell us something, we just did not pick up on what it was.

Totally there were nineteen regular grades assigned and the Officer in charge. Eight of them we were able to identify but Ed and I both agreed we had better not say anything. About half an hour after we got set up the Warrant Officer came to our bunker and advised we should stay inside for the night and he would have his men check the claymores and the wire for integrity. What the hell was that all about?

You could barely see thru the gun ports by now—it was getting dark and Ed said he would call base and inform them of our situation.

This was a usual procedure. One more check of the camp and we could not find the (Vietnamese) warrant officer assigned there—he was just gone! Oh, what the hell, maybe he wandered off and got himself killed. We were then informed that he was around someplace.

Funny, he just disappeared!

For a showplace this camp was a real shithouse, weeds in the wire, crap all over the tops of the bunkers. By the looks of things I was surprised that the .50 cal was still in the tower. Thirty feet up. They were probably to damn lazy to crawl up and remove it or it would have been sold by now.

Ed mentioned we might have to stay over tomorrow and go thru the security of the camp and insure all security measures were in place; wire, mines, guns—the whole place. Another favorite of some of these so called mercenaries was to take the back off of the claymore mines, remove the C-4 and cook with it. It was a constant battle just keeping them in place and operative, and also to insure that some little bastard did not turn them around so the first time you hit the plunger you got your head blown off...a favorite trick of the V.C. and their buddies (relatives) that worked for us.

Neither of us could put our finger on what was going on. Something was not right. Ed got on the radio and informed base that the warrant officer usually assigned to the camp had disappeared. The attitude was "so what"! Business as usual! Ed near shit and told them to inform the G-2 ASAP. I think we both knew something was going to happen.

About that time I said I wish I had a beer! Ed jumped up and almost yelled!

Now I know what's been bugging me. Everyone has new uniforms. Ed said he did not recognize anyone there—I told him I'd seen a couple of them before but not all.

Ed jumped up and said come on Egan let's check out that Vietnamese Special Forces sergeant that was in the bunker with the warrant officer, the one we spoke to earlier.

Ed got right to the point and asked him how long he'd been assigned to Soui Dau. Two weeks he replied in Vietnamese. I asked about the other new faces we'd seen...same answer! Ed and I looked at each other and nodded OK in the affirmative and tried to make it look like we were only curious as we had not been there for a while ourselves.

The dumb bastard bought it. He had no idea we were on to something. Ed asked me what I thought as soon as we got to our bunker. I told Ed I was uneasy from the time we got here. Ed was pissed and for a change it wasn't me who was looking to hang some ass. I could not have been happier. When we get back to base it won't be me bitching to the team commander…maybe then he'll pay attention and do something about the three turn-coats in the camp.

It was dark now but still early and you could look out the gun ports and see spooky was busy and the gun-ships were running in and out of our area now, hot and heavy wonder what the hell is going on. Never could figure out how those guys kept from running into each other.

Not to often did I allow myself to think what things would be like when I returned to the states. I was looking forward to finding out. We had heard that all hell was breaking out on the university campus' around the country and in the streets in some of the larger cities around the country. What the hell is going on. Now they want to cut off funding for the war effort. For God's sake does anyone realize that would be like lining everyone of the soldiers in country against the wall and shooting them. Just say, excuse me, we have to go home now and all's well with the world!! People were going to die and a lot of them. We also heard that it was not safe in the airports for anyone in uniform. So what are we supposed to do? Land, catch a cab and hide! Horse shit! By now I was almost looking forward to some type of confrontation. I thought I was fighting for my country not against my country and I was not going to let someone push me into some corner.

The longer you lay around in some bunker thinking it might be your last night on earth the more perturbed you become. I guess my attitude toward the whole thing right now is—I'll deal with it when and if I get there. I guess all I have to do is make it thru tonight and I'll see the team commander and call it quits.

It was dark now. Not much else we could do now. Ed told me to get some shut eye and he would take the first tour. Said he still felt uneasy about what was going on.

OK. Shake me if you get tired. Time to wrap myself around my CAR15 and nod. All of the sudden—Boom! Sounded like a truck hit the bunker. The road side of the bunker was caved in and it partially buried both of us. Ed screamed Sappers! (A hand tossed "Bomb-in-a-Bag".)

We got hit hard and it did not look to good for us! We were both confused and the explosion did not help our hearing either. Ed grabbed the radio and called base. Go ahead 87 over, what's the problem?

We are under attack. Need light (Spooky), artillery, and anything else you can get, over.

How many? Was the reply! Ed was pissed and said he had no fuckin idea but it looks like the fourth of July out here.

Roger, stand by.

Now would be a good time to start launching some defense. Ed and I both reached for our weapons and started to return fire. All the while knowing this was going to be a futile attempt, but what the hell…might as well take some of them along with us. Ed was now back on the radio with base screaming for help—again! Told them to just get help and stop trying to sort out how many we have down here. One hell of a lot more than the two of us can handle. Just get help!

Base informed us that Nha Trang, 5th group headquarters had been notified and that spooky was on the way…he was already on station in the area and should be about 5 minutes out and try and hold on!

We had a brief lull in the shooting and it gave us a chance to look. only to see what appeared to be people coming in from the North and West side of the camp—in waves. Holy shit Egan we're in big trouble!

Ed got back on the radio and declared a "Prairie Fire". That, simply put was the highest level of a combat emergency. Anything and everything that was in the air and in the vicinity now had precedence over what they were engaged in and would divert immediately to our location…only one hitch…you better damn well be ready to prove you needed this type of assistance. No problem—all they had to do was get a look at our location from the air and it would explain itself and the fact that there were only two Americans down there should be all that was needed.

Base this is 87 over.

Understand you have declared a "Prairie Fire" over.

Correct. Now get them here. We won't have time to come up with our frequency. You give it to them and tell them to come up clear on arrival. We need help and need it bad. Don't fuck around and stop asking dumb-ass questions.

The gun-ships at Nha Trang should be on station by now…they have all worked for us before and are well aware of our locations and the sizes of our compounds. Now all we had to do was hope they got here safe.

What surprised both Ed and I was the fact that our Vietnamese CIDG hadn't decided to run. They were actually firing their weapons…maybe straight up in the air but at least they were making noise.

Ed said Egan, do you think you can make the .50 tower?

Sure. Why not? It was only 75 feet away and 30 feet straight up. Anyway, I like the .50. It was one bad weapon and if you knew what you were doing you could squeeze out more that just the recommended sustained rate of fire…it was a little trick one of the Instructors back at Bragg taught me in weapons training. Of course he was the same guy who told me how to get more distance out of a 4.2 Mortar. Leave the extensions on and put a teaspoon of gas or two in the tube before dropping the round in. If it worked fine. If not who the hell would know!

I looked back and said—"see ya Brown"! In that split second we both knew this was probably the last time we'd see each other alive, but now it's time to haul ass!

CHAPTER SEVEN

(Things do not look good)

Felt like the whole NVA army was outside the bunker just waiting for me to show my head. I've been shot at before, just not so many times all at once. Just do not slow down and head straight for the tower. Five seconds later, bang! I knew I was hit. Damn that hurt. Felt like it spun me in a circle. It was my left leg. I was almost at the tower, dropped my weapon and did not even try to find it the hale of bullets and the darkness. Just make the tower. Damn that thing hurts. Just make the tower…it's my only hope at this point.

I'm there. Rack a belt in this big thing, twist the barrel all the way in and back off three clicks. Now I'm ready. Pull back the cocking mechanism and "rock and roll"! Seemed easy enough at the time, but I was bleeding all over the place and had to tie off my leg. I knew once I started the tracers would mark my position and I would be in deep poop. Boom! I woke the sleeping giant! Here we go, let the damn thing run and hopefully at a sustained rate it would not jam. Now all I could see was what seemed like a thousand Christmas tree lights coming from the north and west sides of the camp. They knew my location. Rounds started hitting the sandbags and the tin roof. Damn, this was not any Viet Cong element I'd ever encountered. There was more to it and I just knew the N.V.A. regulars were involved. Just how damn many I couldn't figure out from where I was at.

I knew now I had to get the hell out of the tower and try and get back down and assist Ed. If we ever got any air support I wanted to be central to what would be left of the camp once the gun ships started to make their runs if they ever got there.

As soon as I started down the ladder, I slipped and fell most of the way and thank God, landed right on top of the weapon I lost when I got hit.

I could here Ed screaming at whoever he had contact with on the radio. As it turned out it was Spooky. I remember Ed yelling we need light now damn it! You've got the coordinates of this damn place, start laying down some fire…we have people in the wire and some of them have already made it into the camp. By the looks of their uniforms they are NVA.

Damn, that was an RPG and I know it was intended for me. This meant they had eyes in the camp and Ed and I were definitely in more trouble that either of us ever considered. Where the hell are the gun ships?

I was dazed and confused. I headed in the direction I thought the bunker was in. It seemed like I heard Ed's voice and headed out—just like before. Haul ass, worse thing they can do now is shoot me again! Was not looking forward to that shit either, but the likelihood now seemed greater that it did fifteen minutes ago and I was hoping Ed was still in one piece.

I hit the bunker screaming. It's me Ed, check fire.

Ed smiled and said shit Egan when that damn .50 quit I thought you were dead. I said not yet. I got hit in the leg on the way out but I'll be alright.

Ed said "put a patch on it man" we got work to do!

I started to look for some type of first aid kit in what was left of the bunker. Patched myself up and even found a surett of morphine which helped—a lot!

Boom! Someone tripped one of the claymores and the pellets were bouncing off our bunker. That means we had to cut the wires on the rest. Didn't dare try and use one of them—they were probably all turned in toward the center of the camp and on us. I told Ed I was going to turn them back out and he screamed no way—if you go out, just cut the wires and get your ass back in here.

Ed was just a little pissed when I got back. He said you're nuts. I told him it went smooth, I think they thought I was one of them. I walked right straight to the berm and started cutting wires.

Next thing I know Ed is popping hand held flares and firing at the berm in the direction I was coming in from. I thought he was shooting at me once. Then I looked back and he nailed somebody pointing at me.

Ed said they are in the wire Egan!

I took one look over my shoulder and spotted something move in what appeared to be some type of poncho. I just sprayed the area and luckily I nailed three of them. Then Boom! It was another sapper squad. One of them pulled the detonator when I shot him.

We both knew the CIDG bunkers were getting hit hard but there was nothing we could do. Did not make much sense to expose ourselves just to prove what we already knew. The flare that Ed popped was just a flicker and once that died we had no more. If spooky didn't start dropping soon it was over for us. These little bastards were a frightening menace and mean bastards. But they were as organized as the old Chinese fire drill. The ones still outside the camp were continuing to lay down fire, but they were now killing some of their own—the ones who breached the wire. Usually that was the job of the Viet Cong that were Omni present with the NVA regulars. Usually we only had to contend with the Viet Cong not the regulars. This was different and neither one of us could figure out just who the hell we were fighting. Not that it made a big difference—they all had guns! But when you are fighting first and foremost the NVA regulars, they never traveled in small "hit and run units": like the V.C. did. Company and division sized elements! Something we really did not want to ponder right now.

Ed got back on the radio and asked where the hell the air support was we had ordered 30 minutes ago. We declared a 'Prairie Fire'. Top priority! About the same time he was screaming at base—Pow! The sky lit up like daylight. It was Spooky—one right after another. Eight Seven, Spooky 517 sorry it took so long what's going on and where do you want the fire to start. Looks like you boys have your hands full. The place is lit up like a small city down there…my guess is a couple thousand anyway, maybe more!

Just what the hell we needed to hear, but we knew he was probably right. He had seen situations like this before and from up there and was able to make a pretty good estimate of what he was dealing with and what we were up against.

We were both so glad to see that flare we didn't give a shit. We knew he was about to cut loose with the cannons (mini-guns) he had on board and there was no escaping the wrath they rained down. When he cut loose it sounded like a cross between a hand held power saw and a bull with his dick hooked on a nail.

Ed told spooky to hit the tree line just to the west. Raise hell and then hit the wire, we've got sappers.

Roger, tree line to west first, then the wire. You got a small camp down there but we've worked smaller areas. Get to some good cover— these things make a mess.

Ed replied. Have at it. Things are not pretty down here now. We need help bad—fuck the mess!

Ed looked at me as if to say "What now Egan"? Lets just lay down some sporadic fire and see if we can keep the ones that are in the camp at bay. I told Ed we had to stay in the bunker at all cost. Spooky has his orders and you know what he does. I told Ed that this seemed a bit much just to get rid of one person…but I put nothing past that damn Major Knock. He knew I was due to rotate and so far he has tried three separate times to get me killed. If we get out of this one Ed I'm going to shoot that bastard on sight. And if I find out anyone else was involved I'll kill them to. This "lose face", "Save face" horseshit has gone too far this time. I'll tell you another thing Ed—if that damn warrant officer who is supposed to be in this camp somehow shows up when this shit is over I'm going to stick a knife right in his forehead.

Where the hell are the gun ships?

For Christ's sake, we cannot hold out much longer Ed.

Ed handed me the radio and said try and make contact with the base and find out what you can about the rest of our support.

Base, 87 over. Go ahead. Where the hell are the gun ships? It's been an hour and spooky is doing all he can, half the team is shot up and we have bodies all over the place.

87 this is base—are both Americans still alive?

What the hell kind of question is that? Who the hell did he think he was talking to? Where are the gun ships and what's the status? Get off your ass and stop asking stupid questions—just do your fuckin job. I knew then that Major Knock was right there in the commo room waiting to hear I was dead.

Roger, we have been in contact with the MIKE force and they are on the way down. My god have you people lost your minds. They can't come in. Spooky is on station and we need the gun ships—no way in hell will they do us any good. They will get themselves killed if they try. Tell them thanks but stay back and clear of the camp. We have enough problems. If we are still in this shit when daylight comes we'll call off Spooky and let them in.

I was not much on radio protocol.

Spooky heard the communication we had with base and came up clear and informed us that from where he was he could see choppers making it our way. I'll make contact with the lead chopper and have them come up now.

Roger that, thanks much, standing by.

87, base. Go ahead base. Choppers enroute. Lead chopper is Wolf pack three zero, copy.

Roger, wolf pack 30.

Spooky, this is 87 on the ground did you copy that.

Roger. Understand I'll have to clear the airspace prior to their arrival and I'll have to stop dropping flares so the boys don't get tangled in the lines when they get here. You're going to be in the dark for a few minutes so stir up all the shit you can once you make contact with wolf pack. You'll probably have a full minute, maybe two in the dark. We'll be on station and monitor everything—don't worry we'll get you boys out of there one way or the other.

Copy, thanks much!

I didn't like it when he said "or the other"!

I looked around to inform Ed and he was gone. I almost shit. I screamed Ed, where the hell are you? He was sitting in the doorway tunnel, sort of an entry way to the bunker, with his usual grin. He said I heard!

Bunkhouse 87, this is wolf pack three zero.

Talk to them Egan. Ed was still laying down fire. This is 87 go.

We are over your position. Two gun ships with a full load 24000 rounds (mini-gun) each and a full compliment of rockets. Ready for fire mission.

65

By this time spooky realized we needed more light and widened his pattern to stay clear of the choppers when he dropped his flares. The choppers knew that the light was going to screw up their night vision but we needed everything we could get. These little bastards were not letting up. They were relentless.

Wolf pack this is 87 be advised that the first heavy fire we took came from the tree line just west of the camp. We now have them in the wire and in the camp. You are clear to fire on the camp. All the good guys are either dead or in bunkers.

Roger 87, understand, hit the camp?

Three one—you copy? Hit the camp. Mini guns and door guns only. Roger, hit the camp. No rockets.

There was a stall and Ed asked me what the hell was going on. Confirm with the choppers Egan. Hit the camp. We're trapped, we can't hold out!

Three one, what's the problem? Hit this damn place! Do it now!!

The choppers are turning Egan, looks like they decided to make the run on the camp—shit! Here it comes. Cover Egan, cover!! Now I know what the VC must feel like when we call it in on them. This time we called it in on ourselves.

There is no explaining what the sound of the mini guns is like…I never really knew until now. This time it's up close and personal. The fading light of the flares is the only light now but when the guns opened up with full compliment it was a giant ball of fire on each side of the chopper and a roaring noise that can never be explained—everything in it's path is flattened and set fire and the ground around looks like the eruption of a volcano. What the hell have we done this time! To late now, let them finish—take cover!

I don't know where Ed is. God I hope he didn't get hit. Ed. Where the hell are you? Over here Egan—I'm OK but I might have to change my skivvies when this one's over!

Always the funny guy! Ed could find humor at a funeral, hopefully this time it would not be our own. I cannot remember a time in my life when I was more afraid. If I ever had plans of going out I'm sure it was not like this.

Damn Egan, here they come again! What the hell did you tell those guys? I guess they are just a little pissed that they got to the party a bit late. Three One, 87 over.

Go ahead 87.

What's it look like out there? We're OK but it sounds like hell down here. Just stay where you are. We haven't finished yet. Going to make two more runs. Both choppers are running low on ammo and we do not want to arm the rockets until we have to. We have been taking some small arms fire but nothing serious. All OK here—nobody hit— Yet! You boys OK?

I got one in the leg. Ed's doing fine. If he's hit he hasn't said anything, but we've been a little busy down here.

87, three one, over.

Go! After we make the last run with the mini-guns I am going to arm the rockets on both ships and unload…we are making our own light now. These guns belch some kind of fire, and I can see what the hell we are shooting at. Should be able to put a big hole in the area to the north then we'll head back to reload and put spooky back on station when we depart. He'll start his drop as soon as we clear his air space—give you plenty of light and keep up as much sustained rate of fire as he can—I've been advised there is another spooky in the air and waiting for a call if needed. Keep you heads down here we come again.

Roger three one. Advise spooky to come up clear when he takes over, we need to see what's left and he can see everything from where he is. Need to know if we have to try and make a run for it….it might just be a last ditch effort. Further, advise the MIKE force on the road to stand ready just in case.

Roger 87. See you guys when we get back. Stay in the damn bunker and keep talking. I need to hear you're OK.

Ed looked back at me and said that's all we need…a lull between the gun ships and spooky. It should give those bastards just enough time to try and make another all out assault on us. What the hell do we do now Egan?

Not much left to do Ed. We'll hold them off as best we can The tree line to the west seems to be lighting up again. Where the hell were they hiding when the gun ships hit that area?

Bunkhouse. This is Spooky five seven one back on station Over. Go ahead, over.

Want us to hit that wire again and then the trees or how do you want it?

It's your party. You can see better than we can from up there. Put it down where you think it will have the most impact and just keep it up. Put out some light so we can keep track of the wire and the area east of our bunker.

Ed and I could hear Spooky and Wolf Pack talking about the situation and we were starting to feel we might just have a chance of getting out of here alive Ed. You got any idea how long this shit's been going on? He said "I-da-know", a week? Still had his sense of humor and we're still not sure when it's going to end. What the hell else ya gonna say when you're up to your ass in alligators and can't find the plug to the swamp. Finally Ed said four, maybe five hours. All I could think to say was "time sure goes by fast when your having fun"! It always seemed like a dumb ass cliché to me, but it fit!

Ed, I gotta piss, how bout you? He just smiled and said "not any more!"

Ed said come on Egan we gotta check out the other bunkers and see if we still have anyone alive.

We both got out at the same time and could now see by the light of the flares what was left of the camp....bodies all over the damn place! We started taking small arms fire from that damn tree line again.

That's it Egan. Get back in the bunker. Give me that damn radio! Spooky five-seven-one. This is bunkhouse over. Go ahead bunkhouse. Want you to make a hot run at that tree line and do not let up until you've expended every damn round you have onboard over. You sure? You damn right, just do it!! After what seemed another hour of spooky working that line to the west things fell near silent. It was actually another fifteen minutes.

Ed had the radio and told spooky to just orbit and keep the light coming...hold the guns and let us check on the rest of our people.

Roger that bunkhouse, we'll be right here if you need us—just give the word! We'll keep the place lighted. Be careful boys.

After just looking around Ed and I looked at each other—dumbfounded! There were bodies all over the place. On top of bunkers—hanging out of bunkers, in the wire...and my favorite, there was one hanging by his leg from the ladder to the .50 tower, about half way to the top, which was eerily, still standing, in the middle of the camp.

We made our way to several of the bunkers. Found two of our people still alive in one and several dead. Ed was checking the last bunker and yelling in English so he would not be mistaken for NVA and shot. I didn't even give it a thought! Funny I had not gotten myself shot. He found four dead and one wounded. He was CIDG. One of ours and that meant MEDEVAC! But how? We hauled him back to our bunker, what was left of it and started to patch him. I knew there was still some morphine which would help.

Ed and I began to realize that the battle might just be over and if we needed help fast Spooky was still on station. Ed contacted Nha Trang and told them to hold the choppers for now and to contact spooky for a situation report. We also knew that there was the MIKE force still on station just up the road. Ed and I worked the camp for anymore survivors—we now had three. Found one more just outside our own bunker. We had missed him in all the foray. Two walking wounded and two that would have to be lifted out.

Now we have to find the rest of our own (CIDG). Move the bodies to a separate area and account for everyone. I hated this job but had done it many times before…I think it was starting to wear on Ed a little as well. He hadn't cracked a joke for five minutes! Ten of our people were dead!

CHAPTER EIGHT

(Body count and cleanup)

Daylight was coming. How the hell long had we been in this mess? I'm not cleaning up any of the bodies this day—way to many and I think Ed felt the same way. All I wanted to do now was find that damn Warrant Officer. I also wanted to speak with Major Knock when and if we ever got back to base.

Finally, Ed got a call from bunkhouse one. The team commander. He was on the way with choppers. Didn't say if he might have any help—just choppers. I guess we both knew there would be the usual photo op crew, like always. They had enough sense to bring an E.O.D. team with them (Explosives Ordinance Disposal). Let them roll the bodies and check for booby traps and make the final assessment of the number of kills. All we wanted to do was get the hell out of there, get a little first aid, something to drink a shower and some sleep.

I told Ed not to say anything about my leg. They would have shipped me straight home. Al I needed was a week or two and I would heal up at the team house. I was coming off the roster anyway. I just wanted to stick around long enough to get a crack at Major Knock. He did not come to Soui Dau. He usually came along with the Team

Commander in situations like this, but he was a no show on this one. Didn't surprise me, it only reaffirmed what I already knew.

When the choppers arrived we contacted spooky and thanked him for the help. Told him to tell the other guys thanks as well. I hope they made it back.

The parade has begun. Assholes from 5th Group Hqs with the requisite half dozen cameras hanging around their necks. Never have figured how they managed to take pictures and kiss the Colonels ass at the same time.

The only sanity that can come out of this is if the E.O.D. team tells everyone concerned to stay (way) back—out of the way and do not, for any reason—touch anything. We advised the E.O.D. personnel of the mess in the tree line to the west and further advised it may be prudent to wait for the Mike force to come in and mop up, but let them know of tree line.

I think Ed told one of the Officers who was armed only with a camera and a bag of film that he might just want to get a weapon in case one of the dead bodies was not as dead as everyone thinks and starts shooting. On reflection that was not a good idea either...the dumb bastard might shoot himself or one of us. With that, the little bastard hauled ass to the dark side of one of the two still standing bunkers.

Now we are confronted by two Colonels and our Team Commander. "What happened men"? My God is the guy blind? All we could hear was the clicking of cameras...It reaffirmed what Ed had said and told them they might just want to set up some type of perimeter guard here as some of these guys might just still be alive! He (one of the Colonels) yelled at the guy that had made it behind the bunker and told him to get a weapon and watch the place...Holy shit, I hope we can just get the hell out of here before one of these dumb bastards gets shot and Ed and I have to explain that as well.

Our team commander asked if we were alright...Ed looked at me and saw me shaking my head and said, Ya, sure! Then looked back at me and smiled. Ed knew I was getting weak and told the team commander to have one of the choppers get us out of there and to have them stop by one of the field medical units just to have a once over and wait and take us back to the team house. Our team commander was no fool, he knew what was up.

The Team Commander said OK guys, see you when we get things accounted for here. We'll make out a report for you if that's OK.. I told him I wanted to know if that Warrant Officer showed up, and if he did that he might want to detain him until he could explain where he went just a few minutes before the sappers hit. Ed said to me that the report would probably not even mention the two of us…and in the same breath said they better not pull any of that kind of shit because I'm going to demand they give us a copy even if it cost me my career. It damn near cost us our lives and they are not going to take that away.

All I wanted to do was get looked at by some medic, get a few stitches, another little shot of morphine and a big shot of whiskey!

The choppers were cool at fifteen hundred feet. The pilot asked if we wanted to make a pass over the camp. Almost simultaneously, "Hell no" was the reply. "We were there all night". You guys must be tired. Get out of here before someone wants us to come back and clean up the mess.

What I cannot figure out is how an element this size managed to slip past our S-2 and all of the Vietnamese military personnel without being reported. Knock lived in the village just outside the compound—he was more like a warlord than a Major in the active Vietnamese military—nothing got past him and anything unusual was reported immediately, but how had this slipped past. My strong feeling is he was well aware and saw an opportunity to get rid of me. I spoke with the S-2 after the war and during the conversation he informed me that he had sponsored Major Knock to come to the states after the war and had helped set him up with a place to live and employment. He caught himself before I found out where he was. All I wanted to know is how and why the incident at Soui Dau took place.

I discussed the situation between myself and Major Knock with Ed. He agreed something was drastically wrong, but also said he was unaware of My Counterpart Mr. Dang at Nui Ti and the W.O. at Sui Dau. He said, Egan, you have got to get the hell out of here—that guy see's you and he'll probably shit, but he will not give up till you're dead. I told Ed to stay clear of me in camp but to watch things until I could make some type of arrangements to clear the area. They didn't get me yesterday, but this to today and it's just getting started.

I contacted the Team Sergeant and told him the situation. He said he was aware of the bad blood, but did not know it had gone as far as it had. He told me to clean up, pack and get the hell in the team jeep when I was ready and he'd take me to Nha Trang. Fuck the report. He would make sure it was correct. He said he was right next to the radio all night and never expected to see us alive again—No one did!!! I said OK and asked him to keep where I was going quiet until I could either find another team in country or rotate. In either case I was almost due to return to the states anyway…maybe a week or two! I was on a six month extension on my original tour so it didn't make much difference.

I never saw Ed again!!

I was on my way to Ton-son-Nhut air base in Saigon within 48 hours. I was on my way home and back to Fort Bragg, N.C.. The leg was sore as hell but I didn't want to say anything. I would probably end up in some field hospital for a week and I couldn't handle that. I'll take care of it myself or check in to some V.A. hospital when I get to the states. I went to the club on the base, hoping to find some medic that was off the clock and willing to look at my leg without raising eyebrows, I was on my way out of country and did not want to end up in some field hospital for any reason. My brother John had rotated back home. I was glad. By the way things were now being handled there I sensed something was not just right, not like the last time when I stayed with John on one of my stand-downs. Things were changing and not for the better! I was dirty and tired and sure as hell did not feel up to arguing with some butt head shave tail just out of the academy. These bastards ran around saluting their own shadow. Leg really hurts. Maybe I'll go to the club and self- medicate. Got to keep my head in some order. I have to find out when the flights leave. War's over for now!!

I took off and went to the Special Forces "safe house" not far from the base here in Saigon. Figured if I stayed around that damn air base waiting for orders out I would only succeed in getting myself in trouble…told the people in booking that I would be back tomorrow, and left with some clerk telling me I could not leave the base. I just wanted to slap the little bastard. I really, really did! I managed to catch a ride downtown with some understanding Colonel who was on his way to the American Embassy. He knew where I had come from and asked no questions, save one: "You on you're way home"? Yes Sir! Well here's your location. Did not remember telling him where I was headed. I didn't! He knew…apparently he had been in this area before and was aware of where we went. He was not allowed in, and he knew it. Good Luck Soldier!

The past few days now seemed like a bad dream and I wondered to myself if it had all taken place, and like once before, I wondered if I was really alive, or was I dead and just being forced to relive some of my past as a penance…maybe there's someplace in the middle for people like me.

Ran into a couple of people I knew at the safe house. They were both on stand down from up north. (I-Corp) CCN- MACV-SOG, and you can bet when they left the area someone was going to be short another jeep. I told them I was assigned to A-502. They asked if I heard about the situation at Soui Dau. When I told them I was one of the Americans that was there one of them ordered another round of drinks and started asking what had happened, which is normal when you run into a dead man walking. They said that from the reports they heard it was a reinforced North Vietnamese battalion…which meant that there were at least 2500 regulars plus the Viet Cong and any sympathizers from the area. My blood turned to ice when I realized there were over 3000 individuals that had tried to attack the camp at Soui Dau. One of them said "you don't look to good Egan", what's wrong? After explaining that I had no idea of the odds or what we were up against they understood. Is that why you're getting out of the area? No I said, and spent the next hour or so explaining my rather tenuous position with the SF counterparts at the team—the Major and two Warrant Officers. Damn was the reply, you are lucky to be alive. What the hell are they going to do about the bastards? I told them probably nothing! The team commander indicated he was aware, that G-2 had known for some time. I guess that means O.K., we know, have a nice life, go away and don't make waves. So, if you are out of the area we can go back to business as usual and the heat will be off. You guys know anyone feel free to jump in…let somebody know what's going on out there. I have a sense the only reason that the same people who hit us the other night would have hit the base camp if that Damn Vietnamese Major had not been there. No one has to bull shit me! That guy's wife was in and out of that camp like she owned the place. No one knew where she came from or where she went. I know she always took supplies with her—food, medical, etc.. The same things we were told to conserve. We had a chief medic there that spent all of his time running in and out of Nha Trang getting paperwork for his lady friend so he could marry her and take her back to the states. She was another one who was hauling supplies out of our base camp like it was a super market....Personally, I didn't think he was a very good (SF) medic. Whenever it was necessary to take one of my people to the dispensary for help all he did was bitch...he'd have to take time, open something or worse yet use up supplies intended for his girl friend and her family, the Vietnamese Major and his family and God knows who else. I really didn't give a shit, I just did not care for the way he waved it under everyone's nose. Also, the G-2 in the camp was more than just buddies with Major knock...counterpart to the team commander. I had overheard talk that when the war was over our G-2 was going to sponsor the bastard in the states...there was just to much bullshit going on there. I guess I really did not care. I knew for sure I'd never have to operate with the guy so I just basically ignored him—like everyone else. I think some of them were afraid of him and for what reason I have no idea. By the time this incident happened I was half nuts anyway and basically felt I could operate on my own if I had to. I sure as hell didn't need or want any of his help.

I was beginning to feel bad about my people at Nui Ti. I knew they were in good hands. My friend Mike was now assigned to the team and he took over right where I left off. He and I did most things alike so there should not be any problems. I only hoped Mike would be OK. He was savvy and knew enough to watch his back and I know he was told about the Warrant Officer (Mr. Dang)! For all I know Mike may just even things up. Mike always did have a way of wanting things neat and tidy. His way!

You guys know if they have any place here a guy can stay for the night? I sure as hell was not going back to that damn air base...I'll check in tomorrow and see if they have my orders and departure date. I hope I run in to that little prick clerk again—I'll lay him out!! I won't put up with some little shit ass harping at me. I don't feel good physically and mentally I'm a wreck!! Why don't you get someone here to look at that hole in your leg Egan? There's probably a doctor in this bunch someplace. Don't know where half of them come from, but they are not all Americans. We know who they work for but not where they come from! Look Egan, if we can help out with anything else before you leave let us know. Get some sleep. We'll be up most of the night and if the leg starts to bother you yell out, we'll do something. Need some painers? I've got some morphine suret's. Here, take one just in case. Morphine suret's were almost standard issue for team personnel. Thanks for everything guys. See you back in the states. Are you coming back? Probably, if I can get a job up north. I want to get on SOG.

(Special Operations Group). CCN preferably. One of them said I could probably go tonight if I wanted to—he heard they were looking for people up there and needed them bad. Thanks, but no thanks boys. But I'll keep it in mind if things don't work out state side. I knew I'd be back.

Went back to the air base the next morning and checked with the records clerk...no orders yet. Come back around 1400, should have another batch by then was the conversation. OK. I did ask if they came in would we be booked out the same day. The guy at the desk didn't know but did tell me he would make every effort to get me on the next flight. He knew I was not going to put up with anything from his crew, all he wanted to do was get me out of the area. Apparently he had experience with our kind and did not want trouble I headed for the N.C.O. Club on the Air base. I hoped no one recognized me from my last trip to the place. I did not feel like talking to any baby faced air force clerks.

My brother who was stationed there had gone back to the states, I did however manage to see a friend of his I'd met before. That's all she wrote! Next thing I know it's almost 1400 and I was half shit-faced, but I wanted to go home and I had to check in. I only walked in the door and the Officer at the desk came up and said Sergeant Egan, we have your orders...can you be ready to board by 1800? What the hell, did he think I was going to say? No!

I was ready to go home, just not ready to listen to anyone tell me what to do, how to do it and where to go. I had a small bag that they wanted me to check in...I said no and that was it. I guess by the look on my face they knew what would transpire if they pushed it! I was given a group number and a flight number, assigned a bus that would take us to the plane and after listening to some of the most insane, asinine bullshit I'd ever heard I simply broke ranks and walked to the bus—again, they knew better than to say anything to me...I was the only one there with the famous "Green Beret" on his head. I was left totally alone. I did however, have to listen to the "war stories" that I knew, for the most part, were coming out of the mouths of the clerks.

Once we boarded the plane there was more of the same. Some self appointed asshole read the riot act to everyone about drinking on the plane. There would be none. What did they think I had in the little bag I was carrying. One quart of good booze a friend of mine gave me at the safe house and no way in hell was I going to turn it in like the bastard chastised everyone to do prior to departure.

What were they going to do? Send me back to Vietnam! I just did not give a damn. I was tired, weak, dirty and hungry—a sure recipe for disaster. I went to the rear of the plane and said nothing! I sat alone. The next stop would be Japan. Maybe I could clean up there. I hope so…I stunk. I knew where I would go. I'd been to Japan before when I was in the Navy and knew of customs there…I knew the protocol in the public bath houses'. Just go in, stay quiet, and when you're totally naked there were buckets of very cold water you poured over yourself prior to going in the public bath. A mineral pool where the water was warm and you could just sit, close your eyes and drift off to another world. A place in the past. A place where you just relaxed and put all else out of your mind—you did not have to understand the language. The looks on everyone's face said it all! What's this dumb-ass American doing here? All the while smiling and jabbering and bowing. Oh, and by the way—men and women in the same pool. Just different dressing rooms! Go figure!

The flight was a little rough but I just relaxed and tried to sleep. This was not to be. Only a few days ago I had been in a situation that most would not recover from. I was wondering if Ed was OK and if he was going to stay at the team, seek other digs, or just rotate. I had no idea when he was due to return home, but I know if it had been any other individual from the team at Soui Dau that night, it would have been over before it got started. I thought of my team of INDIG that I left on the hill (Nui Ti). My interpreter and my buddy Mike. I guess I knew things would be alright but I just could not stop thinking about Soui Dau and the events that unfolded four nights ago. The night that would forever change my life. I even gave some thought to the pilots in the choppers and the absolutely fantastic job they did, as well as Spooky. Maybe someone should write a book some day and call it "Those crazy bastards with the Mini- Guns"! Crazy? Maybe! Hero's all. Thanks guys. They somewhat reminded me of the story in Irish Lore about the "Banshee"! It is said that when you hear the scream of the Banshee someone around you will die…If you see the Banshee, she will throw blood in your face and you will die. The screaming of the mini-guns sounded like the Banshee. I did not see her but someone else did that night. There were bodies and blood almost as far as I cared to look. I was covered in blood…my own. I guess it was a warning.

I got the attention of one of the Stewarts (civilian) that was on the flight. I was in the rear of the plane trying to stay to myself. I politely asked if I could get my bottle of whiskey out and have a drink. A smile and a nod was all I needed. She did tell me to be somewhat discrete as there was not supposed to be any alcoholic beverage' on the plane...I told her I knew and would be careful. After I finished my drink she asked if I would like to have something to eat. I told her no...but thanks, I think I'll have a sleep and asked when she thought we might make Japan. Jokingly she said "you'll finish off your bottle of whiskey before we get there!" I guess she meant at least another six to eight hours.

It was easy to see who the individuals were who had been in combat situations. They were the quiet ones. Most of them trying to sleep. It was easy to pick out the clerks and supply personnel...all loud as hell and bitching about not being able to sleep on a plane. After all, most of them slept in Air-conditioned barracks, on beds with clean sheets every day and ate in mess halls off tables, with plates. I guess after a year of that shit trying to relax in a seat on a plane for ten to twelve hours was a real kick in the ass. Oh, what the hell it won't be long before we land in Japan and I swear I really will find that bath house. I just wanted to be left alone. I had not given much thought about going back to (Fort) Bragg or what I was going to do when I got there. I did know it was going to take some getting used to...I knew in my heart I would never make it stateside. I knew all along I would be back in Vietnam within the first six months back if I made it that long. I have never in my life felt as empty as I was feeling at this very moment...I was really afraid and did not know of what. Kind of like that damn "Limbo zone" the Nun's always talked about when I was a kid in Catholic grade school. You know, the place between Heaven and Hell! God was not ready to have you and the Devil didn't want you! The Nun's dressed and screamed like the fabled "Banshee"! I was in a state of shock for eight years! As I looked back I was probably in a state of shock for the first thirty three years of my life!

I must have finally dozed off and slept for a couple of hours. The Stewart shook me and said I had to put my seat belt on. It was getting a little rough out and it would not be long before we would be landing. I remember too that it was getting light...I straightened up in my seat and recalled someone telling me when I was in the Navy that when you leave Japan if you can see the top of Mount Fuji you will someday return. It was clear as a bell that day and the mountain was beautiful.

Now it is light and we are beginning to make out decent. The pilot came over the intercom and said "we're half way home boys", be landing soon and just in case you haven't figured it out yet, it will be Japan. If you look out the right side of the plane you will be able to see Mount Fuji...It is a clear day and it is a beautiful sight! They were right, I came back. I took the long scenic route, but I came back. There it is—Mount Fuji, beautiful, just beautiful...Majestic!

The airplane cracked and came alive with the Captain's voice. Just to advise you fine soldiers, we will be landing at Tokyo International soon...I have been advised that there will be Officers from all branches of service there to greet you and explain what will transpire. From my experience making these flights gentlemen, listen closely! You do not want to miss your connecting flight home. I do not know if I will personally be making the final leg home with you, but, it has been a real pleasure and a personal honor for me guys. Buckle up, Good luck and God speed!

CHAPTER NINE

(The long and painful road home)

The planes engines began to make that special roar you always hear when they begin their decent...I hear the flaps starting to come down and as we turn on final one more power up to straighten out and Tokyo International is in sight. It is just beginning to get dark and one of the biggest cities in the world with all its flickering lights coming alive seem to cover the earth from up here...some of these guys are a little edgy. Only a few days ago the combat soldiers were looking at the same type of stuff, only it was a lot darker and the blinking little lights were gun fire. This is not going to be as pleasant as I had hoped it would be. I myself am starting to sweat and my hands are shaking. Four days ago I was damn near killed in one of the single biggest onslaughts ever experienced in Vietnam. It was later reported the element was an reinforced North Vietnamese Battalion...in numbers this meant thirty five hundred regulars plus Viet Cong—around two hundred trying to overrun the camp I was in. There were two of us (Americans) and seventeen of our locals that worked for us. We both got out and ten of our people were killed...I guess the sides were just a little lopsided. They probably figured they walked into a trap before it was over that night. Yeah, I am just a little jumpy. The stewards knew I had enough booze in me for six people but it does not seem to be having much of an effect…I'll check out the swamp water in Tokyo. Maybe something will calm me down. I have not seen one of our guys (Special Forces). I guess I'm the only one on board. Don't have much in common with any of the others.

Make sure your seat belts are fastened gentlemen. We are on final decent and will be landing in approximately two minutes. The weather is calm, it is raining lightly on the ground and the temperature is… roarrr, the engines were reversed and the plane jumped a little and then the whining noise, the wheels are touching down and again another roar, the one that would bring this big son-of-a-bitch to a stop. We taxi toward the terminal and the plane stops and a truck with steps approaches as the doors are opened. Once things in the terminal calmed down someone from the military replacement section jumped on board and began shouting orders. This guy must have some kind of death wish. No one paid much attention and if he had not debarked when he did, sadly may have gone over the side of the steps…about fifty feet to the tarmac. There were others in the terminal a little more understanding of what they were dealing with who simply requested that we listen for about five minutes and then would be free to roam around, as long as we did not leave the base. Bullshit, that's all I had to hear! Break what rules? What the hell were they going to do…send me back to Vietnam!!

I will make my own connections, follow my own rules, do as I damn well please, get myself a shower and a bottle of good booze and stay by myself. I don't trust anyone of these people and I damn sure don't trust myself—yet! My leg is killing me!

It was easy to pick out the guys who had just spent a year or more of their life in some hole or bunker in southeast Asia. Just look across the room. Young kids forced to grow up way too fast. Most of them will not even be able to buy a beer legally when they get home. Not yet twenty one years of age most and have already lived a lifetime. Look in their faces and they are blank…scared kids just wanting to go home to their families and crawl into the beds they left that their mothers made up for them, sleep a long while and when they awake pretend it was all a bad dream. I've been watching a kid with his head down for the last half hour not saying a word…when he finally looked up it was easy to see he had tears in his eyes. It could as well been my brother Jimmy but he was home now. Safe. I only imagined this must have been how he felt.

My God! Oh so young!

Then there were the ones in clean, pressed uniforms. Telling war stories to each other. Stories they read on citations for medals that came across their desks in some office. Giddy! They could not wait to get home to tell anyone who would listen just how bad it was, "over there"! What? Only one air conditioner per room. There would be stories from them that would cause the rest of us problems. Simply because people prefer the fictionalized version of things rather that the actual account. They refuse to believe that reality is anything but a made up concoction. I know for sure I'm never going to make it back in the states. I'm ordered back to Fort Bragg. That's the home of Special Forces. The home of the John F. Kennedy Center for Special Warfare.

Now its time to figure a way off this damn compound and head for the Ginza. I had no idea what to expect. Things have grown since I was here last. I was in the Navy then and God knows I didn't need much help getting in trouble the last time around.

I headed for the front gate and was promptly stopped by one of the Military Police. He told me that if I had just come from Vietnam I would not be able to leave the area. After a brief encounter this young pup decided it would not be worth what was about to happen if he attempted to detain me. Never could figure out what just coming from Vietnam had to do with anything…what the hell! Maybe some jerk officer who was in charge in Japan, had never been to Vietnam but was getting credit for a tour was only trying to make things difficult. Christ sake, not another one from the second infantry division. I could only pray that it would be one in the same. I know for sure I would have cracked his skull. The young Police Officer simply said "try and stay out of trouble"! "I'll deny you came thru my gate if you get caught". Off I went. I thought it would somehow make things a little better if I could just be alone the way I was feeling. I caught a small cab and asked the driver (he spoke broken English) if he would take me to a bath house. He obliged me. I did not know it at the time, but my leg was bleeding and my trousers were a mess.

This little guy actually helped me get inside the building and assisted me in getting my clothes off! When he saw the mess he called someone for help. I explained what had happened and asked him not to call the military police. He then sought aid from a man across the street who had an herbal healing shop. They all came inside the bath house, stripped me down and proceeded to soak and wash me with buckets of hot mineral water. They did not want me to go into the bath. When all was finished and my leg was patched I asked where my clothes were. The driver informed me that someone had taken them for cleaning and would be back in half an hour or so and to just make myself as comfortable as possible. One of the people there gave me a beautiful robe to put on. I felt a little embarrassed and calm at the same time. These wonderful Japanese people recognized my plight. I guess it was just their way of life. They were kind and asked for nothing. An elderly lady brought in a tray of hot sake. Japanese wine. It was relaxing. Not one time did I ever wonder for my safety. I had no desire to go any further than right there. I asked the driver if he would express my gratitude as I knew no other way to say thank you. He did and everyone smiled and nodded.

No one asked questions…they just knew.

No long after, my cloths arrived. They were cleaned, pressed and all the medals were on the uniform in proper order. I was beginning to feel better. Not just physically, but about myself all because of them. I knew I would have to leave and so did they, but asked for nothing in return. I asked the cab driver who stuck with me to take me back to the base. It was a slow and enjoyable ride thru Tokyo and on arrival I tried to pay the driver…he refused. I thanked him. It was all that was necessary.

The guard at the gate was different and he asked me where I came from and how I got off the base. I simply stated I did not want any problems and that I was coming on the base and would be catching a plane home soon as I had just come from Vietnam. I wanted no trouble. I think he understood. I caught a shuttle to the cantonment area and checked in. Once again I was asked where the hell I was. I asked why, had I missed something. I gave the guy my name and was told I could pick up my orders and would be told which gate to go to. I do not think that anyone there really wanted to mess with someone with a "Green Beret" on his head. They had all heard stories and wanted nothing to do with the outcome if they got involved. We were damn near untouchable and we all knew it!

I had about an hour to kill and decided to find something to drink. I picked up a quart of V.O. and headed for the can. I was about finished. Had all I wanted to drink when the M.P. came in and decided to flex his power. I told him to go to hell…send me back to Vietnam if he wanted or in about one hour I would be getting on that plane out there and headed for the States. He relented! Once again I managed to call some boneheads bluff! I headed for the gate area. All I wanted to do now was find a corner to sit in and go to sleep for a few minutes. They would be calling us to board the plane soon and I did not want to miss my ride home. I had no idea where home was. I looked at the outside of the envelope with my records and orders and the flight (number 487) was written in bold letters. I guess they thought I was blind!

I was beginning to feel half human again. Didn't realize a short, hot mineral bath, a rub down and some kind of herbal patch on my leg could make such a difference. I guess they knew what they were doing. I looked down at my uniform and the medals and ribbons were all in the right place, the uniform was clean…my Beret as well! Do not ask me how they did all this in such a short time. They just did! Back in the states any cleaner would be glad to do the same thing, minus the medals, probably screw up the job, refuse to do the beret, have it back in four to five days if I was lucky and then charge me only $40.00 for nothing! Oh well, that's what I'm heading back to and I'll be damned if I'm ready.

Another funny thing…they shaved me! I must have really zonked out! I shudder to think about what they used…this was no electric razor shave! Maybe they thought I was dead and were getting me ready to bury.

A crackle of static came over the intercom. Gentlemen let me have your attention…everyone on flight 487, we will be boarding in approximately ten minutes at gate 12. Holy shit! This is gate 20. We were told to wait here and not move. Just like some prick clerk! It'll take 10 minutes to get to the right area. I should have stayed in Vietnam—I could have shot the son-of-a-bitch and got away with it. What surprised me is the almost absolute quiet except for the clomping of worn boots moving to the right gate area. These guys were tired and scared. Most of them (kids) had been screwed with so much in the last year or two all they wanted to do was go home—the one they had as kids, crawl into the old bed, cover up and sleep for a long time…where it was safe.

There is that same kid I saw when we landed. He's still crying and no one is bothering this guy. I found out he is a Marine. Maybe I'll ask him if he knew my brother Jimmy—slim chance, but it's an ice breaker. Possibility he might open up to me since everyone is avoiding me as well. These guys are like animals—they sense something is not just right and want to avoid confrontation—smart!!

Once again the crackle of static on the intercom…I just knew they were about to tell us that we had to return to gate 12. All I said was "boys brace your ass" "if the prick wants us return to gate 12—stand fast, I'll see whoever is in charge and get it straightened out—Enough is Enough!! The voice came up and stated we would be boarding right away, get a copy of your orders out and get in line, they will be checked as you board the plane. I guess they figured someone headed for Vietnam got this far and decided they would head back home! It has happened so I guess this time they did something right. I grabbed the kid and told him to follow me—we were headed to the front of the line. I told him I had an extra quart of booze in my bag and if he wanted a drink to sit by me—in the rear of the plane…I have been this route before and they do not bother you there, and from my experience, anyone with a "Green Beret" on his head would not be bothered anyway. I never did figure out what that was all about but what the hell? I figured they were told not to engage in conversation as most of the people in our organization ran classified operations and it would appear they were trying to compromise one of us and they would get involved in something they did not want to.

We were finally seated—it was hot on the plane—no air yet but it did not seem to bother anyone. It was the final leg of a long journey and all they wanted to do was go home.

One of the stewardess got on the intercom and it was the same old thing about mask, seat belts, water and crash landings etc.. She said "sit back gentlemen and enjoy the ride home". We'll be serving box lunch shortly after take off if anyone is hungry. This is a "no frills" flight. She disappeared behind some curtain and off we went with a roar. Full speed, nose up, wheels up and we are airborne. This seemed to wake the senses. Everyone came alive and let out a big yell. I looked over and the kid was smiling. I asked him if he wanted a drink. He did not say a word. I took out the bottle and handed it to him. He took a big swallow and handed the bottle back…I took a drink and put it away. About this time some asshole said "I smell booze"! I said "shut-the-fuck-up". That was it. I got out of my seat when the plane leveled off and went back and had a little heart to heart with the guy and told him he had best keep his mouth shut for the rest of the flight. Three hundred soldiers on this flight and one "asshole". It is the last I heard of him. I returned to my seat and the kid was sitting there with a smile on his face. I said "It's about time"! I asked him if he by chance knew my brother Jimmy...I told him that he was with the bunch at Khe San and he was wounded up there. I also told him that he was at the Citadel and other places and I was surprised he hadn't been shot a long time ago. I did not mean that in the literal sense, but he got the idea and started to loosen up. He knew I saw him crying but didn't say anything. I guess he thought that made him less of a man. What he did not realize was that made him a man...one with genuine feelings who probably saw a lot of his buddies get killed and was still trying to shake it off. I said "look corporal" you see some of the one's here with the biggest mouths. They never saw one day in combat. Clerks, cooks and motor pool. Worse part is when they get home all their buddies will hear these stories and believe every word. It eats my ass, but don't let it bother you kid—shake it off.

He asked me what Special Forces was all about. Said he heard about us but no one ever seem to know a hell of a lot. I guess you guys just do your job and go home (back to the team house). I said that's about it. We run pretty free and do as we damn well please—rank and file really mean nothing to us. We are all trained the same; officer and enlisted and are pretty much on a first name basis not some "yes sir No sir" bullshit. He said he had heard that and said that must be nice. The plane was now at cruise altitude and the Captain came on the intercom and introduced himself. Welcomed all of us home and said it was an honor to be on the flight...he had made the flight many times before. I guess this was his contribution to the war effort. He got paid, but he also volunteered for the assignment thru his company...I'm not sure who the government contracted with...anyway it was nice to hear his voice. I remember going the other direction and he came up and said we might have to go around as he has been advised the airfield is taking heavy fire and mortars...not this time, we are going home. I looked over and the kid was sound asleep. For a brief second I saw my brother Jimmy again, just sitting there. I smiled to myself and tried to sleep.

I knew it would be a while before we arrived in Seattle (SEATAC) as it was referred to. I was wondering if I should just find a way to go right back to Vietnam or go someplace for a short while…home, Bragg, what? I really did not care just then, I'd make that decision when the time came. I knew I was different from the rest of the Soldiers on that plane. I had fought the same war, only on much different terms… not with other American units, another level, with tribe people for the most part. Hmong's (nungs), jarai, radai…there were several. All good people and they hated the Viet-Cong. They were not well liked by the Vietnamese but managed to get along—they were the fighters, not the Vietnamese. They were lazy and wanted the Americans to do it all for them and when the war was over just hand them the keys to the country. Hell, the appointed leaders in the south during all administrations of the war only lined their Swiss bank accounts and made arrangements with our government to be granted political asylum and be set up for life in the United States when it was all over.

Whatever herbal medicine the people in Tokyo had put on my leg was now beginning to wear off a little and the pain was coming back. Maybe it's just sitting for so long—maybe it's a lot of things…I just did not want to say anything and end up in some Military hospital as soon as we hit the ground. I'll chance it. By now I knew I would have to head for my Fathers place. He would have the local Doctor look at things and I could rest at his place! No hospitals! I also knew I would have to get some bandages and tape as soon as we got in—someplace!

Seemed like we had been on the plane forever. Everyone onboard are starting to get a little edgy, they were sleeping for a while. Now they sense the end is in sight for most of them…the rest of us still have decisions to make. No doubt now, I am going to my Dad's house. I also know that once we touch down in Seattle it's every man for himself.

Once the plane was on the ground there were people to meet the regulars and started directing them to areas they would need to check in…I am on my own! Special Forces personnel carried their own records and orders and had no need for much direction. I'll get my bags, get a ticket and head out. Not quite that simple! With a hangover I was in no mood to fool around as the baggage clerk was about to find out. They lost a cross-bow I had sent back and all hell broke loose! As I went over the counter after the condescending son-of-a-bitch I was abruptly pulled back by the biggest state police officer I had ever seen in my life...he said follow me, you will not get your items back. He been this route before. Nothing you can do about it. Let's just get you something to eat and get you a ticket home. I thanked him, but said I'd rather not eat just now. I looked at him and smiled and asked if he had anything to drink. He smiled back and said no, but I know just the place. We got in his squad car (front seat) and headed for a liquor store. I damn near shit! Me a cop and bottle of booze (on him)! He told me to have a drink if I wanted. I asked if this was a trap and he just chuckled. Nope! I just appreciate what you have done and where you just came from. I'll stick with you till you board your plane home. You won't have any problems with me around...I thought "no shit", who's crazy enough to screw with a guy this size. He looked like Goliath with a gun.

Head of the line it was. They knew this officer, apparently he'd been working this area for quite some time. It was boarding time, I thanked him, he simply said "good luck soldier" and it was on the plane to my Dad's house in Wisconsin. Hope it's warm there. I'm not even sure what month it is. I do not care. I'm going home.

CHAPTER TEN

(Arriving in a wheel chair)

I thought it would be easier to get back home. By this time you would think the process would have the kinks ironed out and logistics in place to make the transition out of Vietnam smoother...not true! The individuals that processed us out of Vietnam never spent one day in combat!! The idiots along the way were the sons of politicians and were getting credit for actually being in Vietnam...True! Acting like horses asses came natural for them. They had nothing to worry about. If they were to get in some kind of trouble Daddy would come to the rescue and you can bet some poor bastard other than them would suffer for any misgivings.

Now on the final leg of a long trip I was getting just a little edgy and asked the stewardess if I could break out my bottle. She said go ahead, you are not on a commercial flight. If you want anything to eat just ask. If you want anything else to drink just yell. Biggest mistake she ever made in her life! By the time the plane landed in Madison I had no idea what country I was in. No shape to try and navigate off the plane under my own power they called for a wheel chair...off the plane I went on the cargo elevator and into the flight crew quarters. By this time my Dad and Uncle were looking for me and thought I had not made the flight—or worse. They finally got someone at the gate to check the flight roster and found out I was in fact on the plane but not able to walk they almost shit. They thought for sure I was wounded—well, I was, but it was not what kept me from walking under my own power. I was shit-faced!! Thanks to the flight crew! I guess the Green Beret gave me away and they were very accommodating. By the time they got to me they were frantic but after determining the situation, laughter was in order. I finally woke up enough to see my Dad. We both smiled and hugs were in order. When I finally tried to stand I was feeling the pain in my leg again. They thought I was kidding until they looked and saw the blood. Tears came to my Dads eyes. I reassured him I would be alright and not to involve the Military authorities or the V.A. as they would call me back for evaluation. Dad said he would get me to a Doctor as soon as he could. We stopped about twenty miles from the airport for a little bracer! When we finally arrived home Dad called the Doctor. The Doctor turned out to be his best friend (Doc.). Doc was a dentist and every bit as good as any medical type. Doc actually gave a shit and did not try to flex his ego, like some of the little pricks at the V.A. Hospital. The interns as they were called Things have changed exponentially since that time. He just dressed my little wound wrote a prescription for some painers, said "there—how's that", you owe me five bucks, (he was only kidding) and the rest is history.

That night I finally managed to get some rest...I did not sleep much. Still thinking of what had taken place in the past week or so. I wanted to tell someone but figured what the hell, no one would believe me anyway. I really did not care. I was thinking about my interpreter and his family. The guys on the hill at the outpost I left behind, and my buddy Mike. Funny how things went for the two of us. I knew in my heart that Mike would be OK and that he would take care of the team. I sensed it would be the last time I would see him however. Nothing I could do now, that part of my life is over but I keep getting this naggy feeling I'll be going back...Maybe not to the "A" site but to another Special Forces assignment someplace in country! Woke up several times during the night with cold sweats fully expecting gun fire, choppers...something, anything! It was too damn quiet.

I woke my Dad and said lets go for a ride. He said it's the middle of the night! I said I cannot sleep Dad I just need to get out—go someplace, anyplace! Just go! He said O.K., hold on while I get dressed. I thing he understood. I know he did. He knew that someday he might have to face this very thing with one of his boys—just not so soon. I'm sure it reminded him of things he would rather have forgotten.

After an hour or so of just roaming around the back roads I guess I fell asleep. When I woke up we were parked on the front lawn of the house. Dad said you can sleep in the car if you want or better yet the front yard, I'll toss a blanket out if you want—I'm going to bed! He made me smile. It had been a long time since I was able to do that. After all these years I was beginning to understand what Dad had been going thru since our Mother died. He just wanted to go back and start over again with me…I knew it in my heart, I just did not appreciate what he was trying to say. I should have known. I had taken everything for granted all these years and felt sorry for myself. I suppose being in the famous "Green Berets" went a long way in impressing him and he was proud, but I was wearing the damn thing just a little to tight and it was starting cloud my judgment. I woke up the next morning to the sound of Dad banging on the door of the car where I finally passed out. I damn near tore the inside out of the car and pee'd myself at the same time! He said "come on man, your home"…time to snap out of it, things to do. Breakfast is on the table and you can cut the grass when you finish! I said I hope you have a nice quiet riding mower. He knew I had a half ass hang over and reminded me of what he made me do many years earlier when I was a kid and came home half in the bag and woke up with what I think was my first hangover. Holy Balls!! He made me stay home from school. He was putting in a new drain line for the sewer and was digging out the ditch, by hand. I was put to task finishing the job and swore I would never look at another beer again… only this time I think he wanted me to dig it up! He laughed his ass off and said he was just kidding but there were people coming to visit and he wanted me fed, sober and clean…yes sir, he was proud and I felt good about that. It was a long hard bloody road, but it was worth it.

The first one in the door was Doc. I was glad of that, I liked him and he asked how the leg was. I jokingly asked if he was going to bill me for a house call. Once again I saw my Dad smile. All this was beginning to stir emotions that I had not felt in many years. I loved Dad…I was just afraid to tell him. He knew.

I told Dad that I just wanted to sleep for a few hours. He told me to go ahead he would make sure it was quiet. I said "not to quiet" or I'll never get to sleep. He smiled again—he understood!

When I finally woke up I was wet, like I had been in a rainstorm…Dad asked me what I was screaming about? I said I have no idea. He added that he could not understand a word I said—it was some foreign language…I said Dad, where the hell do you think I've been? Ireland!! He knew right then and there that my life would never be like it was…he saw himself. In that instant I suddenly realized what he had been thru all the years since both his wars. I felt shame. Myself, like many others get the idea no one understands. They do, it's just hard to relate, since their war was so long ago. We did not understand what our fathers had been thru because we never took the time to ask…we were to busy with our friends to even care, and then, like now, led to the feeling of self pity, drinking, depression and in some cases—suicide for some soldiers. As I observed, Vietnam was not going to be any different. Why should it.

I knew that I had a few days before reporting to Fort Bragg and I had no idea what to do until then.

I phoned an individual in Washington, D.C. that handled all of the assignments for Special Forces personnel…we all had her number and made use of it. I told her I would probably be going back to Vietnam but I would have to go to Bragg first which seemed like a waste of time and money. She agreed and said stay close to the phone for a few hours and she would see what she could do. I did not realize that Dad had been listening. He asked me if I was nuts, and as quickly said "don't answer that"! What the hell are you thinking? Do you want to get killed? It scared my Dad and I saw that empty far away look on his face…kind of like the one he had the day he received notice he was being drafted back into the service and would be going to Korea. If I had only known. I had no idea it was tearing him up inside. I made the call for my own selfish reasons—I was not finished yet. Maybe I was trying to get myself killed, but I'd do all the damage I could on the way. My fire in the sky was getting brighter and I was riding a flaming chariot straight into the sun. I had no fear of dying, it was getting there that was starting to tire me.

I told Dad that I had to stay close to the phone for a while. He said he overheard and asked if I wanted a beer or something else to drink. There was plenty on hand at the house. We just sat quietly, across the room from one another, not saying a word.

We were both half in the bag when the phone rang…It was my contact in Washington. She said I would have to go to Bragg first. Sign in and basically—sign out. She would send my new orders there. As screwed up as things were, about now it made sense. Someone had to know who and where we were. I only worried I would end up saying the wrong thing to the wrong person and it would all end. There were actually types (officers mostly) who had not been to Vietnam and would never be going. It was political—they enjoyed the make believe world they were living in and one can only imagine the war stories when their "tour of duty" was over! Fact! At the same time it pissed them off. They were assigned to the replacement outfits in Japan, Hawaii, Kuala Lampur. Myself, like many others just enjoyed doing what we were trained to do and in the process leave everything and everyone behind. The mission was primary.

It was time to enjoy what was left of my mini vacation. I need to get Doc to look at my leg again. I want the damn thing healed before I go back to Bragg. There will be the usual post mission physical and then turn around in a matter of maybe two to three days and get another pre-mission physical.

For the next couple of days all we did was visit family and friends. Everyone wanted to know about Vietnam and I had a hard time telling them. To relate the mayhem and killing would only make it seem like all other wars. I was a victim of the "Green Beret" syndrome…Special Forces. By now everyone had seen or heard of the movie about us and it made us stars—not soldiers like the ones everyone knew of. We were different and no matter what was said it would only cheapen the image. There were dissenters. It was the 60's and the anti-war sentiment was building. I did not want to speak with anyone. I only wanted to go back. It was all I knew. Our unit was small and there were not that many of us. By the time I left country the word was out that many of the "A" sites were getting hit hard and a lot of our guys were not making it out. Hell, I damn near bought it but it only seemed to reinforce my attitude. I am still thinking about my buddy Mike. Mike was a good soldier and we were a lot alike, that's why I knew the team would get along well with him—he was damn well familiar with the ambush areas in our sector but our jobs came with no guarantees, and Mike knew that to.

It would be tough leaving my Dad but I would never tell him... God knows I wish I had.

When the day came to go back to Bragg things were quiet. Dad felt in his heart that he might never see me again, he knew that it would not be long before I was back in Vietnam. We left for the airport that afternoon and it was a somber ride. Not much was said...just be damn sure it's what you want before doing something really dumb. I told him I would. He knew damn well I was only trying to appease him but it didn't stop the tears when I finally boarded the plane...what the hell was that all about? Dad finally softening up after all these years! Maybe. Bragg was just a pit stop, a formality. Pretty much just check in, call Washington again and let them know I was ready to go back. Things were really in a turmoil at Fort Bragg. Seemed like no one knew what was going on. I remember checking in and the first sergeant saying "are you gonna stay?", or are you like the rest of them? Going back! I told him I would probably hang out for a week or two and in the meantime I would call Mrs. "A" as we referred to her. She handled all Special Forces assignments in Washington. Good! Was the reply! I'll schedule you for a post- mission physical and a pre-mission physical all on the same day and you can leave as soon as you get your orders—as a matter of fact if you want to go back on leave I'll send the damn things to you—this way I will have one less of you maniacs to worry about! What the hell did they do to you people over there? No one listens to a damn thing they are told. They do what they damn well please and come and go like this place is some kind of Country Club!

I could see that the first sergeant was not doing well...I felt sorry for him! It's what they do with good soldiers just before they retire, only in this case it was more like a punishment. Kind of like being the warden on devils island.

Got word my orders were in (3 days) and I had to have a pre-mission physical. Got that out of the way same day. No one said a thing about the post mission that I missed. Guess they figured I wouldn't make it back this time so what the hell!

The first Sergeant Told me I could leave anytime. Want to go straight to Nam or do you want to go back on leave. I told him I could not put my Dad thru that again and I would just head for SETAC and leave country as soon as they could arrange transportation out of Pope AFB and if it was possible straight to Seattle.

Mission accomplished! I was scheduled to be at Pope AFB the next morning at 1000 hrs. I packed what I had and signed out, got a ride to Pope AFB with a buddy of mine and he and I spent most of the night at the NCO club…God knows I was ready to go back to Vietnam—where it was safe! My body would not take another day in the states. I remember calling my Dad that night. He picked up the phone and said hello! I said Dad—it's me! Do you have any idea what time it is? Was the reply. Then there was a long silence…he said "you are going back aren't you", I thought it might take a little longer—maybe a week at least! Why? I could not answer that question, I just knew there were tears in his eyes. You had to know that Dad felt he would bury another of his kids before he died. Sure he had a few to many on occasion—he earned every drop.

CHAPTER ELEVEN

(Another bridge—No time to sleep)

People seem to think there has to be a logical reason for doing what appears to be something really insane...like going right back to a war (oops) conflict. Why not? I did not have the slightest idea what the hell it was all about anyway but it did give me the freedom to do the things ordinary soldiers would end up in jail for, it got me out of the standard regimen, that was required in some state-side unit...even Special Forces! Hopefully this little foray will last a few more years and I'll either get sent home in a box or in a straight jacket. I do know that there are groups of individuals in the States (a mixture of college drop outs, drug addicts and pricks to lazy to get a job and not a big enough set of balls to join the service and try and do something from within), protesting in the streets to stop the war...(opps), there I go again—it's a police action, conflict, or some damn thing!! But it is not a War!! There are politicians who seem to be in a weakened state and in fear of losing their jobs in Washington and are bending to the demands of mobs. These individuals want the soldiers pulled out of Vietnam right now and are not giving one thought to how this is to be accomplished except to tell elected representatives to cut off funding! What the hell kind of thinking is that? It is like a high stakes poker game—when all but one is broke everyone goes home—broke, pissed off and dejected. But this is war…call it anything you want—It's War! The protestors think if the funding is cut off and there are no more munitions, everyone just goes home, leaving behind a landscape of broken and dead bodies, inhumanity beyond description and even greater despair to come in the wake of aftermath.

The same individuals seem to think if they shoot the messenger it will all go away. These same individuals believe all banks should be closed if there is a robbery…therefore there can be no more robberies. In this instance they are right, however, not much else will be accomplished. Like I said "shoot the messenger"!!

From what I was able (or even cared to) observe during a couple of brief stints back in the states during the war…all of the protesting originated on the college' campus' throughout the country I love. What appears to have been some social and political studies project gone horribly awry. I was greeted at airports by individuals who were dressed like street urchins, sporting beards and hair that appears to not have been cleaned or trimmed for months. Too some degree I did fear these people, but as a soldier I was trained to not let this type of thing bother me to much…maybe I should have. Myself, like many other of my brothers were confronted and choose to not walk away and in some cases where intervention by the authorities was necessary we were escorted to safety or to jail. It would all depend on the politics of the police. Some would side with the protestors others with the soldiers just trying to do their job. The real professional police knew the feeling of being attacked just for trying to do a job, no more, no less! Things seemed to be getting worse on the home front and were not getting much better in Vietnam.

I knew in my mind that I would trade it all for just one day back on the farm, when I was a teenager, going to school during the day with raging hormones and working hard to get the chores done long after dark when the school day was over and the bus dropped us off. I remember thinking I would someday be in the military, wearing a fancy uniform and have the admiration of adults in the town I came from, who, for the most part, I would rather piss on…and that included the kids of these upstarts. I was now beginning to realize what politicians really did for a living… how they manipulated their constituents, and why. Not one of them had ever been in a war zone. Some had been in Service but were able to find clerical assignments on some reserve base close to home. These people were classified as (Era) veterans. In during the time, not the place! There was another really sad aspect to some of these types…they managed (political) assignments to Officers-Candidate-School and after six months of training were assigned to Infantry units where they managed to ruin the careers of more than one (real) Vietnam veteran, especially any Special Operations Soldiers they encountered. We were totally un-conventional…this is they way we were trained. Much to our own dismay it included being somewhat undisciplined in the area of military courtesy. I am sure these individuals had heard of us and were out to make a point whenever they could. Sad, just plain sad. They know who they are now and after these many years have had to live with their mistake. There was only one of these types that I crossed trails with and to this day if I ever see him I will punch that son-of-a- bitch in the mouth, I do not give a shit where it is or who he may be with.

I remember the day I signed out. The first Sergeant only smiled. He said "for what it's worth, I'll miss you". I think it was his way of saying, we probably will never see each other again. Good Luck son! By the way, I've got a jug in the desk. Want a short one before you leave? I did, and with that one of the guys hauled me over to Pope AFB. It actually adjoined Fort Bragg but was separated by a fence and command. When I got there I went to base operations and checked in and was informed it may be another couple of hours before we left. I could go to the club and check back in if I wanted.

I was getting a little hungry and knew they did not have any food on military flights and it would be several hours before I could eat anything. I had a beer and a couple of burgers. Ran into one of the guys from the 5th and we were both leaving on the same flight. I asked him what he was going to do when he got back. Said he was going to SOG, CCN (Special Operations Group—Command and Control North). I told him I was going to try and get back to the old team but the prospects looked dim, as I was told they were going to close out A-502 and turn it over to some leg G-5 outfit. Here's some candy, here's some cheap cloths. We are going to win your hearts and minds in other ways. If they thought that getting rid of the A-sites and establishing this kind of bull-shit was going to accomplish anything, they all must have a death wish. If not I was going to see what was available up north or possibly at the Delta Recon. I knew a couple of people there and if they were still around I could possibly get in. If not I'll just hang out at the 5th Gp Hqs in Nha Trang for a week or so and just piss people off. He said I should see about going to CCN, they are looking for replacements up there and the area is still as hot as ever. The Ho Chi Mihn trail is starting to fill up with troops and from all the intelligence reports indicate the North Vietnamese Regulars are starting to move south with a lot of equipment. Try as they may the bombing runs just did not seem to be doing much damage and the teams at CCN were going across the border in an effort to see what was being moved in and how. A couple of the teams were detected and were wiped out. I told him he was a piss poor salesman but I was going to look into it anyway. I told him I was going to hang out at the "safe house" when we got in and see what was available there first. He said he was going straight into Nha Trang and get orders to CCN. We agreed we would probably meet up later.

Wouldn't be long now…heard the cracking of a voice on the intercom indicating we would be loading out for SETAC in an half hour. Time to get back to the war where things made a little more sense.

Military flights were definitely the lap of luxury, but somehow seemed more like home if that makes any sense. Maybe it was the regimen—"Sit down", "Strap in", "here's a box with a sammich", the pee tube is in the rear and if you have to do anything else good luck we'll be there in four or five hours, six if your lucky. Then some load master, with a big grin says "your guys going back to Nam? Now I know its time to drop off and get comfortable in the web-belt style seat I'm on—but it's comfortable and I'm tired. Mentally and physically. I'll group my thoughts when we get to Seattle.

I'll probably end up in CCN make a trip of two over the wire and then if I haven't pissed everyone on the planet off I'd like to look into one of the weird operations run out of Saigon. Seems a little confusing, but it's not. We all pretty much operated the same way. They used us where we were needed for a specific reason. Very small teams were the usual concept. Easy in—move fast—easy out! Move on.

The way things are going in country (and at home) right now it will be touch and go for a job. There was word that they are cutting back on all the teams and in general all over the country. That only means one thing—the North will begin to move south and all hell is going to break loose. Our people will get hit hard and the regular army units will take heavy casualties In the classified areas it means destroying records and equipment, keeping it as quiet as possible and when it's time to leave, just leave. Any of the individuals that worked for us will be at the mercy of the N.V.A.. It is simply the way it works. Even if you know for sure, you keep your mouth shut. That kind of information in the wrong hands will get you killed!!

Fasten your shoulder harness boys, we'll be landing in approximately ten minutes, once we land stay on the plane until we are directed in and the tail gate in lowered Blam, just like all the other times—we are on the ground. Pick up your brief case and wait instructions. OK gentlemen we are on the ground—thanks for flying Air Force Airways Look forward to seeing you again. Watch your step. What the hell, everyone has to lighten the load somehow and a little levity never hurt anyone. The return flight on this thing is probably in a body bag. On the flight back in country I was beginning to feel this might be my last trip.Just did not care.After all the shit I had observed, the people involved. I had seen to much. Dealings that were better just left alone—to many powerful individuals involved.

Time to head for base operations. There is usually an Army representative in the area and hopefully, if the dumb bastard is sober maybe he can arrange for transportation to Nha Trang, Special Forces base Headquarters. I just know in my heart things have not changed and I will end up doing it myself. Pretty simple matter. Just head for the airstrip and basically hitch a ride on the first thing heading up that way. First I want to go to the safe house downtown in Saigon and nose around. It's a place where certain of Special Operations personnel hid out when they needed a place to cool off or were on stand down. I know I shouldn't but I'm still curious about where all that damn money is going and why. Get in to deep and I may take the secret to my grave with me. I knew about a printing operation they had in the Philippines for making this supposed counterfeit money...at least that's what I had heard when I was still at Bragg. The Psychological Operations personnel were not that tight lipped and I have a feeling that this whole idea of maybe, just maybe print some bogus and some not so bogus originated there as a lark and it got out of hand. Since we were printing the South Vietnamese currency right here in the U.S. Mints, why then would it be necessary to print bogus money elsewhere for use in some phony operation in country with the intent to destroy the economy. I've got to find out more. Something else is going on. I guess I managed to be in all the right places at

Bragg when this was discussed and no one figured I'd ever get caught up in one of the transfers and try and put it together—or at least wonder what was going on. I did not much care until the incident occurred with our team commanders counterpart Major Knock. To much started to happen after that and it all seemed directed toward getting rid of me. After the incident at Soui Dau is when it all hit me. There had been three separate attempts on my life leading up to that night. Now it is bothering me and I am going to find out more I just do not know how.

Excuse me Sergeant..you boys got anything headed to Da Nang or Nha Trang? Short flight to Nha Trang leaving out in about one hour if you want on stay here, we could leave sooner. O.K., which plane? This one he said and I just went onboard and sat down. He asked if I had just got in country and I explained this was a return from a short stint in the states. He and I made small talk about things in the states and both agreed that there was total confusion at most if not all of the combat units at home. A lot of them had been advised there was a major cutback on the horizon and others said that we were getting ready to launch a major offensive and were all getting ready to ship out. No one seems to know for sure but it is keeping us busy. We haul small amounts of unknown material out of country and they we bring small amounts of something else right back. No one knows what the hell our cargo is and are advised not to ask…just load and unload. Funny thing is we make short hops all over in country doing the same thing prior to leaving. I guess he felt comfortable talking with me since the Special Operations personnel were all into weird shit anyway and probably thought I was part of what was going on.

OK then, it's off to Nha Trang. Hook the belts, they will keep you from flying thru the side if we have to abort on takeoff. Off the ground with no trouble and I was told we'd be in Nha Trang in an hour or so and would not be serving food or drinks, just sit back and enjoy the flight. I laughed when he said that and this guy was standing there with a big grin on his face. Once again I was told if I had to go to the can, there was a pee tube at the rear.

I must have dozed off. The flight master jabbed me and said we were coming to Nha Trang. He said we take small arms fire thru here occasionally, so tighten my seat belt, pucker up my ass and get ready to land. He advised that I should be able to get a ride to Group Headquarters. There is always someone from our outfit there when we touch down. The engines roared and the tires hit all at once and we were in. Short taxi and the gate was opening at the same time. I thanked the guy and he was right, there was a jeep from group waiting. They seemed surprised that I was the only one onboard. I introduced myself and said lets go. First thing out of his mouth was "want a beer"? Sure, why not.

Not far to our compound, it took about fifteen minutes. I started to see some of the people I knew and asked if there were any jobs at CCN. You bet, but are you crazy they are getting hit constantly up there. By the sound of things all I have to do is check in, let someone know where I want to go and I'll be on my way.

When I checked in the personnel officer told me someone from Saigon had been asking if I had checked in yet and I was to contact him prior to assignment at CCN. The personnel Officer asked me what the hell I was getting into. Apparently he had known of others they were asking about for the same reasons. Not much more he could offer. I told him I wanted to be assigned to CCN (Command and Control North) MACV Special Operations. No problem there but he did ask why I was not interested in the people from Saigon who were asking about me. All I told him is that I wanted to leave today for CCN and there was no more discussion—he mumbled something about all you guys are the same, think you can do whatever you damn well please. He also knew better than to push it any further...I told him I would be taking my records with me and all he would have to do is flag an empty spot in his files and mark my name on it and the CCN designation. End of case and it's off to the airfield and hitch a ride to DaNang.

Got anything headed to DaNang? One leaving out in twenty minutes if you want a ride, its that big gray thing out there with the engines running, the tailgate open and the wings full of holes—Good Luck and thanks for flying "Swiss Cheese Airlines"!

I had flown on these things many times, the old C-130. I've jumped out of enough of them at Bragg. Great plane. I believe it would fly on one engine and one wing. Shakes like hell and it's a noisy bastard but all in all a great aircraft. I also think you have to be half Looney to pilot one of them, but then, look where we are. It also helps to have a flight crew of a like mind! They looked more like Pirates.

You know the drill. This is a short flight so there will be no food or drinks served enroute. Strap in. If we get hit on the way there are no soft landings so unhook, bend over and kiss your ass goodbye, that's about all you will time for.

About that time the tailgate began to close and the plane was moving to the ramp, short run up and its wheels up. Hard climb out to forty five hundred feet, level off and hold steady. The air was thick and you could hear the engines stressing. I was told the flight time was about two or three hours. It would all depend on any evasive action we may have to take. Another comforting statement!

Someone was shaking me. Wake up, we are on approach and will begin our decent in one minute, be on the ground in ten. The pilot advised your unit that we have a passenger for them and will be waiting when we land.

Wham! This big sucker is on the ground. They do not waste time coming in. One of the flight crew told me the same thing I had heard in NhaTrang. Things were getting hot in the area. Unless you were some brain dead clerk it did not take a genius to figure out something was going on. Something way out of the ordinary was taking place. I sensed it when I landed in Saigon coming back.

The plane was slowing down as we headed for the off-load zone. The tailgate was coming down and I could see the jeep from MACV Special Operations. Won't be long now.

You Egan? Yup! Get in we've been expecting you. You must be nuts asking for assignment here. One of the guys said he knew you and vouched for that fact. Said you been around a while. There's a place for you to bunk up but we have to stop in at Headquarters first and get you checked in and then we'll stop by the club—it's the coolest (air conditioned) place here and most everyone hangs out there—beer's cold and whiskey is cheap. I noticed coming that we have towers at the gate and more than just the usual security as well as a million miles of razor wire. I see we are dead on the beach and why so many gun towers? This is a small compound! Yes, and when all hell breaks loose we'll be the first ones that gets hit simply because of who we are, the types of operations we pull. The shear level of security tells people we have something to hide. It's a bastard getting in and out of this damn place until they figure out who you are, so be advised. Some of the new people that get assigned up here get a little pissed—mostly officer types, but they get the wind taken out of their sails right after they open their mouth the first time. Don't know where some of the pricks come from but they don't last long. Can't afford that kind of shit here.

When we get you checked in don't be surprised. There are some real great guys at Headquarters. The SGM is a shit head and the Colonel is a real prick. The Sergeant Major is a fat black guy who always has a cigar stuffed in his mouth. He is Omni present with the Colonel. My opinion at the time is they have something to hide and I'm not the only one around here that thinks that—just be careful who you strike up conversation with unless you know them.

The security in this place would make Fort Knox look like a public campground. The boys in the towers are Chinese and do not mind using the guns. Just be careful. We also have Laotians and Cambodians here in small groups for obvious reasons. Don't let it concern you unless you get assigned to one of the teams that use them. They are real touchy about outsiders and right now that's what you are. They will get to know your face however. But until then stay clear. What the hell did I get myself into this time.

This camp had been wiped out during the Tet Offensive and many of the American advisors were killed and all of them wounded. I knew most of them from Bragg or on one of the other teams. They were all fantastic soldiers. Don't know when the decision to rebuild came out, but none of the original people were assigned. I do not know how some of the Officers assigned there ever got into special forces and must have been given a free pass in most of the training—what I saw was an embarrassment. The G-2 (Security) officer was not unlike others in the same position I had met. A real horses ass! After speaking with him which was part of the check in procedure, I had the feeling that he had heard of me and was going to try and make my life miserable. Big mistake! That's what a reputation will do for you. If they don't understand you or cannot find out anything about you—they fear you! For Christ sake, where are all the real people? Where did all these little ass- holes come from. Up till now rank didn't mean a lot at the team level.

It didn't take long. Once I got settled in I got a call from Gp. Hqs.. Didn't seem like much out of the ordinary. I thought it was pretty routine. The Sergeant Major introduced himself. Said there wasn't much going on right now, and asked if I'd mind hanging out and giving them a hand. Strange statement! He went on to say they were reorganizing and were going to get rid of the Laotians that were working for us...

to much trouble, to many problems and no trusted them and went on to say when the reorganization was over he would see about getting me into one of the teams when a slot came open!! What the hell was that about...I was told the people here were short handed on the operational side and I could get to work right away! I found out later that others has sensed the same thing and said something was wrong up there.

CHAPTER TWELVE

The ALPHA and The OMEGA

I was about to learn the toughest lesson in my life and it was going to be handed to me on a real dirty plate. During the next few weeks I sat around just like everyone else, doing nothing—nothing that is, except watch the Colonel and the Sergeant

Major run around together, in and out of the compound in a Black Car that seemed like a status symbol to them. Didn't ask, but I'm sure, like everything else in Special Forces, it was stolen. It was a real piece of junk and never did work right. He had one guy whose only job was to keep it running and it was a full time job. On occasion the Colonel would manage to get out of the compound without the Sergeant Major. When that happened he would sit around and do nothing but sweat, smoke cigars and drink. He was always nervous about something. I always wondered why the Sergeant Major and the Colonel carried their personnel files with them. Their briefcases were "never" out of their sight! I asked one of the other people that worked in the area why they did this. I was told for my own good—don't ask!

A couple of days later I was off the compound and at the Air Force Base just down the road—I was told they had a good hamburger there at one of the clubs if you knew the right people. I had just pulled in and I spotted the Colonel there as well. He had that damn car of his and was talking with someone in plain cloths standing right next to the car. I pulled over, he didn't seen me. I watched and he opened his brief-case for the guy. Damn! There appeared to be gold watches and money! American money, and lots of it. What the hell is going on? Am I the only one in country not running around with a bag of money. After I saw this, I remembered what I had seen months earlier. Counterfeit money my ass! There were a lot of people involved and I knew this would be a good way to get myself killed if I opened my mouth. I realized that a person can know to much. I waited until he left the area and hoped he had not seen me. I drove my jeep to the club, had a beer and left. By the time I got back the Colonel was there. He spotted me but never said anything—I just know he saw me and now it was going to be a cat-and-mouse game!

Finally, when I was not expecting it, one of the team command-ers came in and asked if I would like to pull a mission with him. Easy answer! He said it would be in the North (Vietnam). That's what we were there for. The Colonel was informed and he almost seemed relieved to get rid of me. I know he was aware I was asking questions about him and he was getting very uncomfortable. I was new on the compound and he was running it with an iron fist and in Special Forces that a big no, no! I was told by one of the people that he, the Colonel was extremely paranoid and suspicious of any new arrivals...so what-ever he was doing it had been going on for quite some time.

The Captain told me to inventory my personal belongings put them in a box that was issued just for this purpose and put a mailing label on it. This was a new one on me and when I asked why, he told me that if we did not come back what's in that box might be the only thing left of you and sent to whomever you have on that label. It's stan-dard procedure for anyone who goes over the wire. Usually they don't expect them back.

Once the team is picked for the mission it's off to isolation, where you will stay until launch time. Here is where special weapons are issued as well as uniforms. Choice of the team leader. In this case it would be North Vietnamese uniforms. I promoted myself right on the spot to second lieutenant in the North Vietnamese army. The mission is explained and we are given the target. The type of insertion—one, two or three choppers. Day. Night. You choose the time for the launch and which chopper your team will be on. All five of us. Our choice for the insertion was a "nightingale". A new piece of equipment that would be dropped in ahead of the team. It replicated the sounds of a firefight. I have no idea who came up with this bright idea but we might as well have sent them a letter and let them know we were on the way. The Americans had tried every psychological trick in the book, none of which fooled anyone, and as we were about to find out was not going to work this time either.

We do our job…knowing the people we hunt are in wait at the jungles edge. Makes no difference now, no turning back. The roar of the blades on the chopper signal our arrival. Jumping off you look about knowing we are being watched…it's to late. You spot someone in the bushes ahead and you shoot instinctively. You have found your mark and the hunting is over for one man and a little more of your soul leaves with him. As I look up I see the sun, high in the sky, so why must we warm the ground with blood? Warriors must not allow this thought. It makes little difference now but one day the flowers will grow again.

This mission is not going to go well. The choppers are in flight and clear of our position. I hear dogs. This means "tracker dogs"! Its just a name for wild dogs that have been trained to kill. There have been reports of up to twenty or thirty at a time and now we have to deal with getting shot and ripped to shreds. Get on the radio and call for an extraction, now! Nothing else we can do. Run and hope for the best! One of the chopper pilots radioed in stating he could make it back. Get to high ground and try for an open area. Let me know when you have me in sight. Roger that was the reply from our team leader. Will try and make the ridge just southeast of where you put us in. If it's a no-go try and circle and fire up the tree line at the bottom of the ridge and if you spot any of those damn dogs wipe them out! They are worse than the regulars. Copy that! Haul ass boys, things are going to get a little dicey—I've got you in sight and there are dogs and people right on your ass. Keep moving. I'll separate that bunch and come back. Might have to charge you boys overtime and mileage for this run. We are about to get swallowed up in the bonfires of hell and this guy is making funny. I always thought the chopper pilots were just plain nuts. Flying around in a big green Superman Costume with a blade on it. Right about now I'd settle for that mean bunch of pigs I had to slop on the farm and as each day goes by I wonder more about the strange world of Special Operations; willing to give all for some romanticized version of heroism, and wondering how some of the idiot officers I have run into up here ever got accepted into the army let alone Special Forces. Some of these guys were just plain cowards, there is just no other way to describe them and I strongly suspect some of them have never been thru jump school. Notwithstanding, the Captain I am operating with (the OI) on this trip is a real Straight shooter, (pardon the pun) knows what he's doing and willing to take suggestion without bruising his ego. We are both of the same mind right now; we want to get home alive. He's a Jewish guy and likes to kid about it. In his words "he's got chutzpah"! A "Mick" and a "Jewish rebel"! What a combination.

I know what the mission was all about…at least what we were told in the briefing. I asked the OI and he hesitated and simply stated it was a trail watch—no contact, mark troop movement and the physical numbers and report. I knew we had no contact and the only way that seemed possible is when and if we ever got out alive. We did have transponders. These were activated when we wanted out or got our ass in trouble. Only good for about fifteen minutes talk and forty five minutes tracking. If this failed your ass was in big trouble! In this case we lucked out.

We have you in sight boys—better pop a panel just to be sure. We know you have on funny uniforms, but identify with panel. Roger, will do. Good its you, we are coming in. Tell that damn door gunner to get his finger off the trigger until we are on board. Roger that. Get your team on as soon as we come in—no time for stragglers and we aren't coming back. If I looked anything like the OI just then it must have been a look of terror. The team is on the chopper…. Lets get the hell out of here! I told the OI on the way back I wanted to talk to him after we were debriefed and got cleaned up. I said something is wrong and I have to get this shit off my chest. He said OK and we had a long quiet ride back to base. I had a feeling he knew what was going to come to surface.

Two days later I ran into the Captain and he knew we had to talk. I think he felt I had forgotten about what we had discussed briefly just after the last mission. He was afraid for his career—understandably. He also knew if any word of what we discussed ever got out he was finished—I assured him I would never talk with anyone but I had to let him know of my suspicions. What he did not understand was the reason…and for a long time I did not either. What the hell did I get myself into this time?

For Christ's sake…what counterfeit money? That was the response from my (captain) buddy! I explained that I had been in touch with G-2 at different levels along the way. He was getting edgy. Now what. How the hell does he think I felt. If the people that sent me here ever found out, I was a goner! There was more gold being floated out of the country than there was being traded on the "New York Stock Exchange". The gold was being purchased to destroy what buying power there was left in Southeast Asia. The Asian currency was not being minted in the U.S., but rather in small off-shore (out of the way places), set up by the U.S., therefore, giving us the deniability factor if and when it was even needed.

There was one big problem. The U.S. absolutely needed some counterfeit American money to cover the trail just in case it was ever discovered we were doing this type of thing. Now there are ton's of currency being floated into the Vietnamese economy and nothing to back it up. Once the printing days were over the individuals running the presses decided it was time to get rich and began making (good) money—and only God knows how much but many, many people got very, very rich on the spoils. Probably the most well guarded secret in history.

I tried to avoid him for the next few days…just to test the water. It was not long before I was called in and I figured it was over and now would be the best time to call Saigon and request to be pulled out, but like a damn fool I played along. I was informed there was a mission coming up…that it involved (going in to) Laos. It was a set up! I never saw it coming. These bastards (the SGM and the Col.) had suspected there something was wrong—why I ended up the target is a mystery to this day.

When someone is in deep enough no one is to be trusted—as I was about to find out! I think my arrival may have triggered some suspicion the two of them had for a long time.

Awarding of medals, other phony documents in select officers' records had been going on for some time as well as large sums of money that were being skimmed from mercenary payrolls. Special Operations had large numbers of Vietnamese, Laotian and Chinese personnel working for us and the exact amounts paid to these individuals was highly classified. Each month—after these people were paid, the record was destroyed. I know, I was assigned to a burn detail and this is where the payroll transactions were destroyed. I was reading one of the pages and some asshole officer stopped and said "just burn it", "what's there does not concern you"! Talk about people watching people.

Somehow, the Colonel and the Sergeant Major had collaborated and were successful in in this venture. Skimming off (large) amounts of each months payroll that was (usually) picked up by one of the line officers in Nha Trang each month and the funds brought to Da Nhang for disbursement. This was not the case here however. The Group Commander—the Colonel himself would make the trip. He simply went across the street to the Air Force Base in Da Nhang, caught a plane and he would be on his way to pick up a (cash) payroll for our mercenaries and take his skim on the way back and if it did not work out that way he would stay on the AFB for the night and come back when it was safe the next day after he had taken his portion and this is where things began to change. He spotted me—it was coincidental, but he thought I was watching him…I was simply in the right place at the wrong time. I went to the AFB up the street from our compound to get a burger and spotted him making some kind of transaction, I know he saw me and at the time I did not put it together. Within three days I was called in and informed that I would be going into Laos for the sole purpose of setting up an outpost! What the hell was that all about?

There was no reason for this one—for God's sake!

At best it was a suicide mission, and at worst it was a suicide mission and that bastard knew it! This was a bad situation. This bastard was ruthless…Laos is the one place you could lose someone and get away with it. We were not at war with Laos, (my ass) we were just not supposed to be there and therefore we were not. Plausible deniability!! Like I said, a good place to get rid of someone—at any cost! Just ask "Tricky Dick" (I am not a crook) Nixon and his henchmen. I guess this whole damn thing was about to catch up to me. I thought I was here to fight a war—albeit, I had not the slightest idea what the hell it was all about. I really didn't give a shit. I had no idea that survival was going to be from within. I was real good at what I did, I just hadn't figured on having the punkin turned inside out.

Once the team was organized we were called to the isolation area and briefed on the mission. Not one thing made sense and the other

American assigned to this fiasco asked me if I had been told anything prior to the briefing. I told him no and he said he thought he was losing it…maybe he had been in country to long, but this was bullshit. Have any of these bastards ever been up north? There was no intelligence and you just do not say here we go and expect things to happen. There was no reason for it except they had to get rid of me. I had seen to much. I did not tell him. He was one of the best and if anything happened you would want him at your back. On arrival at the site no one could believe it. The top of a mountain in the middle of nowhere—in Laos! Even our team of mercenaries looked at us like we must have missed the intended spot. Time to dig in and say a prayer for the pilot that got us here. I know that one of the first things we were told to do was clear a landing area for supply flights. Supply what? Who? To this day I still maintain that we (me) were not supposed to come out alive. After we got set up we managed to get a message to base and inform they could bring the supplies in as planned.

The following day a call came in that choppers were on their way and make ready to unload as fast as possible. When they arrived I was shocked to see the Colonel that sent us here and his ass kissing buddy the Sergeant Major. They refused to get off the chopper and the (Black) Sergeant major was turning a bluish grey. How he ever got in to Special Forces is beyond any comprehension. He was a real chicken shit and as I was to learn years later from a friend assigned to a post in Washington after the war, the Colonel had papered the walls with medals. The Colonel was later assigned to a post in Washington after the war and his records were open for scrutiny…this bastard had never been to Jump School (airborne training), therefore he had not been thru any kind of formal training at the John F. Kennedy Center for Special Warfare (Special Forces Training). Everything in his records was paper. It was about to catch up to him. The officer that put the squeeze on him was one of the one's the Colonel shit on in the past. All I know is his medals were stripped, and he was forced to retire.

When you survive a setup things are never the same. After a month on that God forsaken mountain I was ready for just about anything. By the time we were replaced by a new team and returned to Da Nang things were beginning to change. The Colonel was gone and most of the officers that had aligned themselves with him were starting to kiss every ass they could. All in hopes of rotating as soon as possible without their respective records being examined to closely or getting caught up in some mess the Colonel left behind. It was fun watching these guys. Heavy drinking among this bunch was beginning to look like an Olympic event. I don't recall who replaced him but I'm told he was alright. The object was to nail the Colonel and any of his cohorts. Don't know what happened after that. Did not much care. When my time to rotate came around, I was notified to report to Saigon for debriefing and then it would be back to Nha Trang....there were some people there I had to see before departing. Things were beginning to change, and not for the better. My old team had been disbanded and the guys were spread all over the country and assigned to other A-Sites. The area was turned over to G-5....civilian reparation teams. These guys were all legs and had no idea what was going on in that area and not one of them were combat soldiers.

Think about it. Once the "A-Team" was pulled out of the area, there was no activity from the Viet Cong or the N.V.A. (North Vietnamese Army) regulars. Back to business as usual....you can bet some "horses ass" in an Office in Saigon was saying "I told you it would work"!! Just like the time during the TET Offensive of l968 when the same people in Saigon said "we have had no activity reports of weapons being smuggled into the city"...no reports of increased movement of personnel, therefore, there were no weapons! They paid no attention to the increased numbers of funeral processions the Saigon area either. This is how the Viet Cong and the N.V.A were smuggling weapons into the south. These people billed themselves as the "intelligence branch". Another group that probably held ninety percent of their meetings at some club and would hemorrhage blood if a loud bang came within earshot, and kept a basic supply of "huggies" handy. It was sad, but no one trusted the Intel reports from Saigon. It was safest to trust your own instincts and whatever any of the locals might send our way. Or you could always do like I did...report intended location for the night and move to safer ground. Certain individuals were not happy with this but it worked. Just one more reason why certain persons in the chain were not to happy with me. I'm sure most, if not all had me on their "bucket list".

I still wanted to make another trip to Saigon before I left country. The "Safe House" in Saigon had a lot of it's own secrets and was always a place to go any time you were in Saigon. If you knew the right people there was always something to do. Some type of special operation and they were always looking for people in Group who had been in country and especially from MACV SOG. It also helped if someone would vouch for you. Even if I don't get a chance to see them before a short trip to the states they'll be there when I get back.

Not many familiar faces at Group headquarters in Nha Trang... the ones I knew were like me—all we wanted was to be left alone, process out and go home for a while. A couple of them were really in bad shape—and I thought I was a mess! I discovered one thing. I no longer had any feeling toward people...I was numb, cold and uncaring. I swear, could have watched someone die while I was eating a bowl of rice and it would have no effect on me. It was frightening. What the hell has happened to me? I was a shell. With the latitude we had and the types of missions it's a miracle any of us made it out and I suddenly realized it was not over yet. If I'm going out its going to be in a ball of fire.

CHAPTER THIRTEEN

I really hope no one screws with me on the way back—I'll just keep to myself and be quiet as I can. This is generally where the shit starts with me…some prick trying to flex his power and position in replacement outfits in and out of country. Not me, not this time. They can scream till their balls fall off—I'm going home and I'm coming back.

I realized while sitting by myself in Nha Trang waiting for orders for the states I would never, if at all, come all the way back home and I would face the toughest times of my military life. I had heard there was turmoil in the streets at home. Now what? I leave one war behind and must face another right in my own front yard. I'll never make it once we land in the states if what I've heard comes true. It was not just the young causing all the problems—it was individuals of all ages and they were taking out their (political) frustrations on the soldiers leaving for Vietnam and the ones returning. In the streets, at the airports throughout the country. Everywhere! Yelling, cursing, spitting and getting hit with umbrellas from some of the older ones. Did the authorities actually think we were going to just walk away, not say anything. It was a very dangerous situation and people were getting hurt. Many good soldiers went to jail over this. Some lost their careers and not one thing was said to the instigators.

Checked in at Group Headquarters and was told that my orders would be ready in the morning and that I would be leaving for the states out of Saigon. It was up to me to arrange to get there. A little nervous, a lot apprehensive and wondering if this was the right thing to do. What the hell—go home and try and stay out of trouble, spend some time there and then call Mrs. "A" and let her know I was ready to go back… it's what most of us in Special Forces did. She (Mrs. Alexander) was our go to person in Washington and the one that handled the records and assignments for all special Operations personnel.

The next morning I was reminded that I would have to get to Saigon on my own. Big deal! The Air Force base was less that a mile away, but some of these people couldn't get to the latrine without someone holding their hand. I was handed my records and a clerk was about to deliver a speech when I just walked out…for all I know the little prick is still standing there!

After checking in on the flight line I was told they had something leaving out in half hour. Great! Time for one last blast of whatever at the club. Sure wouldn't want to show up in Saigon sober.

Managed to get a few free ones when everyone at the club found out I was going home. Most of them were Air Force. These boys earned their money to. Again they all warned of the political situation back home and to avoid it at all costs. Like that was going to happen. I thanked everyone, grabbed my bag and headed for the plane. One of the crew jokingly said—Saigon? I said yeah, like there was someplace else. He said sorry there won't be any in flight meals served today… the stewardess is out sick. There's a pee tube up front if you need it. This is a BYOB flight, so strap in and make yourself comfortable. Drink-em-if-you-got-em!

I thought most aircraft were noisy, but the C-130 has a special roar all it's own, especially with the loading ramp down. Here comes the crew. Everyone talking to the flight deck and making hand signals. Up comes the tail gate and we're off. Whoosh! I didn't know that big S.O.B. could move so fast. Five minutes after take off one of the flight crew came over to me and asked if I was OK. I said yeah, why? He said we started taking small arms fire shortly after take off. That's all I needed. I broke out the bottle and one of the crew just smiled. I handed it to him and he said thanks, but I'm on duty! No shit!! If I had to fly this thing in and out of this shit hole, I'd be blind drunk all the time.

Back to Saigon. This time it will be brief. Check in, get a boarding time and place and head to the club if there was time...balls, all you see around here is people in clean uniforms running around like they are in some mall. Everyone saluting and smiling. Seems like there were ample numbers of second lieutenants enjoying getting way to much respect from anyone they could find to force a salute. I've been reprimanded for just the opposite on more than one occasion...what the hell, we just did not do it in our organization and it becomes habit. None of the ones I ran into were about to call me out.

My plane was due to leave in about three hours. Ran into a couple of our people at the club and both were going home on the same flight and all agreed this would prove to be a fun trip as we would probably run into some son of a bitch on the flight home just waiting to flex his rank...God, I hope not! That shit happened on the way home last tour. It does not take much to shut the mouths of these types.

As each day went by I had sensed I was preparing for the last days of September to wrap her arms around me, where the heart begins to warm even in winter and occasionally you allow yourself to feel something and make yourself ready for a place in the ever so growing field of beautiful stones. I was called out and asked if I still had an interest in something new—new to me? I had to make arrangements to cancel my trip back to the states and get new orders. I had to go back to Nha Trang and was told they would be advised and would have new orders for me as soon as I got there. Stayed in Nha Trang for the night and spent most of it in the club. September would have to wait. I would be assigned to an organization few people had ever heard about. This was of my own choosing however and about to be the end of days as I had known them.

The next few days were a whirlwind of activity and briefings.

I could not believe some of the things I was being told. I really did wonder at one point if this was all a joke...what was being discussed was way out of the planning stages. It was a matter of picking the right people for the job. The individuals in charge obviously knew way more than they were letting out to the average units of any branch of service involved in this damn war. It was probably the reason it all seemed just a little exciting, beyond the pale as it were. Special Forces people were used of crazy assignments—some a little more so than others. That's probably why this one, to me, seemed just a little out of the ordinary. Never for one minute did I wonder what would happen if a person said "hold on", this one's not for me! I can speculate. I do know that I would not have seen the light of day until the mission was complete.

My records were taken from me and appropriate personnel notified of my status. It was the last time for along while I would see my personnel file. What this mission was about and the outcome I have never discussed with anyone nor will I disclose the nature of it. Suffice it to say, these are the particular types of operations Special Forces were involved with—quietly!

The horrors of what occurred to certain of Special Forces soldiers is just not worth writing about—it serves no purpose other than dredging up feelings best left alone. Few places or situations in any war can ever describe "man's inhumanity to man". The one's never discussed in the safety of some war room, only alluded to. Not one Officer in his or her right mind making the military a career would ever discuss the ugly mess we had gotten into. No, and they cannot be blamed, after all this thing would someday come to an end and memories would blur—new wars are always on the horizon making dim the prospect of anyone asking why before we start anew. It makes little difference now. It is time to go home. This beautiful jungle will never be the same and as always, peoples of another race will hate us—but that's war—or is it?

I ask not for any explanations. It is not my right. I am a soldier first and foremost, it is my job to obey the orders of the officers above me and thank God for that. The onus of the aftermath lies squarely in their laps. As Special Forces soldiers we were trained to do a particular job and we did them well. Somewhere along the line we were labeled the "Silent Warriors". I guess that's better than being called a bunch of maniacs that run in a herd with a mob mentality.

Usually we worked in tandem with others of the same ilk, avoiding the larger army units and basically having nothing to do with them....we were shunned like lepers!

EPILOGUE

Leaving the country of South Vietnam would prove to be an arduous, time consuming, screwed up mess…dangerous, with little or no planning whatsoever. After all, the individuals in charge had no time to lay on the logistics. Ten years seemed like it would be enough time to plan a complete withdrawal and deal with the materials that would be left behind and Vietnamese personnel that worked for the U.S. Government. You know they would not be welcome with open arms by the new government that was fast crawling up everyone's ass. All at one time there were thousands and thousands of Soldiers from the North Vietnamese Army descending on every province south of the D.M.Z., they were reinforced with Viet Cong regiments. It was about to become a slaughter and someone better damn well hurry.

The last bastion of hope was the roof of the U.S. Embassy building in Saigon, where, what Americans were left were departing from by helicopter…if there was any room left any Vietnamese national who could hold on, to anything would be taken aboard and out to the deck of the Navy carrier waiting in the gulf. Fortunately for myself, I had left country earlier and did not have to witness the carnage.

Was this really a surprise to anyone? Hell no. There had been dissident, pot smoking morons parading up and down every major street in every town in the states for many months. Election time for politicians was on the horizon and not a "ball" in the house! Not one of them gave one rats ass about the soldiers in harms way—only their re-election bids. Politicians of the time were prostitutes with rubber spines. That made them extremely agile and able to bend in whatever direction the wind was blowing. Actually, all of the soldiers I spoke with had more respect for real prostitutes.

One must only go back to when it all started—in the 50's. Naturally it involved the French. We had been cleaning up every mess they made since WWII. There was some ray of hope for the French with the resistance, but their soldiers were, well let's just say they left a lot to be desired!

In the beginning of the War, all of the people of my sort (Special Forces) were sent in country on passports and wore civilian cloths?? What the hell was that all about. The "John F. Kennedy Center for Special Warfare" at Fort Bragg, North Carolina was beginning to train as many Special Forces soldiers as could be in a short period of time… and believe me it took time. Individuals who, first volunteered and then had to be screened prior to being trained in whatever specialty they choose, along with a minimum of a secret clearance. It was specialized, it took time and not everyone made it. Like their predecessors—the first units carried passports, wore sterilized uniforms and began to set up A-Sites throughout the country. Things were building up and losses were being reported. For God's sake these early individuals are the ones who had to hire the mercenaries that would stay with us till the end. Albeit a mess, at least the Special Forces were of the type that had the sense to get the job done without the regimen of other units. Special Forces, the quiet warriors! Not much left to say about the best.

Over the years, I have chosen to be left alone and certainly not involve myself with any Veteran Organizations. Please do not get me wrong—they are great and help soldiers and their families when and wherever they can by directing them to service organizations and the Veterans Administration. Often times some of the clubs end up being just a place to bitch and drink…not for me! Don't get me wrong, a stiff glass of good old "Irish" never hurt anyone, however, I've heard all the war stories I can take. I guess venting thru an alcohol induced fog is alright in some cases. Me, well I'd just as soon go to my Priest. Sobriety not required, but recommended. He's probably heard it all anyway but now it's just the two of you and offers more serenity than the local "honky-tonk" and chances are you'll probably not end up with a fat lip.

It is difficult to put things in some type of perspective. Relating fact based fiction is a way of releasing some pent up anger a person builds up over many years of just listening to some real bull shit. Stories that would melt your heart coming out of people who never saw one day in combat...There is a difference between being in Vietnam and being in service during the Vietnam war. It made them "Vietnam Era" veterans. What a load of shit! It got to the point I wanted to scream. I've heard other vets say the same thing. I will now ride the soft warm winds of September to that place where the carved shiny stones hold the names of Combat Soldiers.

I will now ride the soft warm winds of September to the place where the carved stones hold the names of Combat Soldiers.

CPSIA information can be obtained at www.ICGtesting.com
Printed in the USA
LVOW01s0415050615

441245LV00013B/148/P